UNLEASH YOUR INNER BADASS

WAY OF THE COBRA

By SEAN KANAN

An Imprint of FLiP Creative, LLC
Los Angeles, CA

ISBN 9798591211790

Editing and Book Design by Michele Kanan
Cover by Jason Gonzalez and Michele Kanan
Author Photo by Jim Warren

FOREWORD
By Darryl Vidal

~ Ju Dan
- 10th Degree Black Belt Kenpo Karate
-Inventor of the Crane kick

DEDICATION

I dedicate this book to you, my reader. You and I are cut from the same cloth. We are seekers, looking within ourselves to improve the world around us. Unafraid to accept our faults we forge ahead along the path of self improvement.

To my Wife, Michele

You are my WHY, the magic which inspires, drives, and guides me to be my best. You are my everything. Thank you for my beautiful life.

Have you always wanted to be stronger? More inspired? Reduce your anxiety and confusion? You need a way forward, a plan for the future, an attitude of positivity and a recipe for success! Learn the Way of the COBRA!

Very few movie franchises can claim a "universe" going back as far as the '80s, and extending into the 2020's. Fewer of these have feverish followers of the characters' opposing philosophies that are debated daily in social media as in the Karate Kid / Cobra Kai universe. Dating back to questions whether the crane kick really would work, to the drum technique and why Mike Barnes fell for the Kata, fans have rabidly argued their perspective of the Miyagi Do vs Cobra Kai battle of opposing philosophies. Now with the resurgence of martial arts mystique borne from the latest epic series Cobra Kai, the Way of the COBRA reveals the path forward.

You remember him, screaming, "Your karate's a joke. I own you!" Mike Barnes was truly driven, and it wasn't just an act. Detailed by none other than Karate's Bad Boy, played by Sean Kanan, *Way of the COBRA* provides the reader with insight into the true life of the man behind Daniel-san's major nemesis from Karate Kid III. Much of Mike Barnes' attitude and philosophy can be drawn from true-life experiences of actor, author and producer Sean Kanan, also known for his roles in daytime television, AJ Quartermaine and Deacon Sharpe. But, little did you know that Sean's personal life challenges and philosophies, carried him through life threatening injury, and possible catastrophic failure, to be one of the most successful actors, writers and producers today, highlighted with his most recent #1 selling book, "Success Factor X" and his Emmy success producing and starring in "Studio City."

Over the years, Sean and I have shared our common interest in Eastern philosophies, the rigors of training in Filipino Martial Arts (FMA), and the secrets of our own philosophies and personal life challenges. Sean's continued contributions and dedication to training through his life and career prompted his induction into the martial arts Masters Hall of Fame in 2019. *Way of the COBRA* is Sean's recipe for success through the application of the Strike First, Strike Hard, No Mercy mentality, balanced by self-discipline, self-sacrifice, self-realization and moral rightness! You can learn the *Way of the COBRA* to guide your journey to success and self-satisfaction! Start reading now!

BELTS

WHITE BELT

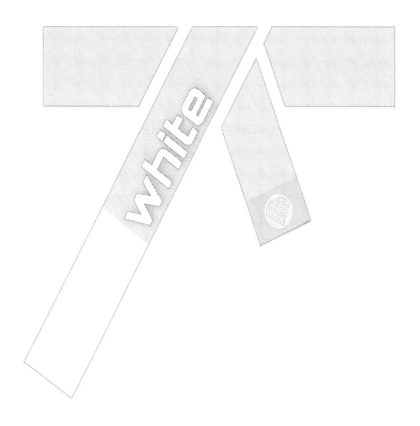

INTRODUCTION

"Success is the ability to go from one failure to another with no loss of enthusiasm."
                    - Winston Churchill

Welcome to my dojo; the dojo of life... COBRA life. I am your Sensei. Time to release your inner badass using my battle-tested tactics and time-proven strategies. Time to wake the beast. Trust me, you have one! It may have gotten lost or ignored for too long, but it's in there. By the end of this book I am going to find that successful, focused, driven COBRA within you. What you do with it is up to you. I recommend becoming a Sensei yourself to guide others do the same. The endless circle of helping yourself by helping others is the *Way of the COBRA*; transform yourself and you can transform the world.

Respect must be earned and I intend to earn yours. I'm just a small town boy with a dream made possible by the Way of the COBRA. My COBRA philosophy propelled me into icon-status as Karate's Bad Boy Mike Barnes in *The Karate Kid III* then saved my life in a near-death experience. Recently, my inner badass co-authored bestseller *Success Factor X*, co-created and starred in the Emmy® award winning TV show, *STUDiO CiTY* on Amazon Prime (which earned me a nomination for Best Actor and best writer) and I lost 35 pounds, all in one year! I share this not to impress you but to impress upon you what is possible. Together we will reveal your path by exploring your personal truth, obstacles, and motivations to charm your inner COBRA out of hiding. I'm up for the challenge... are you? Let's begin.

I've got good news and bad news... funny how it always seems to work that way. If you're like me and Don Corleone, from *The Godfather*, you insist on getting the bad news first. Here it is: I don't have the answer. I can't give you a silver bullet to magically transform you into someone who is successful, focused, confident... you know, a badass.

Now for the good news: The answer already exists inside of you. It's like the Zen riddle: How did the ship get in the bottle? It was always there. The answer to creating the life you want already lives within you. You may be experiencing tremendous success right now. If you are cashin' checks and snappin' necks that's awesome. But if you feel stuck and frustrated; that's even better. I'm going to show you how to harness those feelings, smash your limiting beliefs and rocket yourself into positive change, but you must do two things:

First: Accept that you were born a winner.

How can a baby hold it's breath under water? Success is encoded in our DNA in the form of basic survival instincts. In order for the human race to persist, we have been hardwired to survive... which is the most basic form of success. Cavemen managed to live for over 200,000 years while ducking apex predators like Sabre-Toothed Tigers. But where are those prehistoric, ferocious felines now? Just a footnote in the "book" of human success. You represent a chapter in that "book", so make it count.

Second: Accept responsibility that where you are, is who you are.

Now, repeat out loud: *WHERE I AM IS WHO I AM*. Excellent. Every decision you've ever made, (the good and the questionable) brought you to where you are right now, this reality. You have no one to blame but yourself. However, blame and victimhood have no place in this dojo. Accepting responsibility for your decisions allows you to reclaim the power to change your future.

You may not realize it but you already possess two very important qualities in your favor. If you are reading this book because something isn't working in your life, then my friend, you have *Emotional Intelligence* (self awareness allowing you to recognize there is a problem) and Faith (the belief that change is possible). I take the faith you are placing in me very seriously. So, if you have been depressed, dispassionate and unengaged in your life, it's time to shake off the dust of mediocrity, throw on your black, sleeveless gi and get to work.

You can read all the books in the world about success and motivation but without action you are wasting your time. The rewards you seek are directly related to the effort put into this journey. Completing the writing and exercises in the pages ahead with honesty and thoughtfulness is critical. This will determine your success, identify your *Why* and clarify your goals. Then it's up to you to achieve them.

Congratulations on making the first of many new, proactive decisions that will unleash your inner badass. You have just crossed the threshold taking the first step to becoming a COBRA. Get excited about the future because the future starts right now. Thank you for the opportunity to do what I love, what drives me... inspiring people exactly like you. Now bow to your Sensei and prepare to learn...

WAY OF THE COBRA.

Sincerely,
Sensei Sean Kanan

WHO NEEDS THIS BOOK?

"STOP TRYING TO FIND YOURSELF,
YOU ARE NOT LOST. INSTEAD,
DEFINE YOURSELF."

- MICHELE KANAN

This is the **admit-the-problem** section. Time to get honest with yourself. Don't feel picked on or judged and especially don't quit. No one is watching so don't worry about looking silly or dumb. What have you got to lose besides that lippy inner critic in your head that's making you miss out on massive success and unending happiness? Fear not, we'll regulate that little punk soon enough.

After reading *"Unleash your inner badass"* in the introduction you thought, that sounds like a good idea. But wait... why? If it's on a leash, it must be there for a reason. Yes, there's a reason; someone is hindering your success. But who? Wake up and smell the coffee! If you have to ask then it's you. It's called **Self-Sabotage**. It's a thing... I promise and it's not as uncommon as you may think. It's defined as preventing yourself from reaching your goal. It kills your confidence and wrecks your self-esteem. Are you a self-saboteur? Take this quiz to find out.

- ☐ Have you "failed" repeatedly?
- ☐ Is the voice inside your head a creep?
- ☐ Do you give yourself a treat several times per day?
- ☐ Do you over-eat regularly?
- ☐ Do you have piles of... well, anything in your bedroom?
- ☐ Do you feel stuck?
- ☐ Do you bathe sporadically?
- ☐ Do you have a dealer, a bookie or house account?
- ☐ Have you been rudely "over-served" by a bartender this month?

If you answered "yes" to any of the questions, then let's be honest, you probably answered "yes" to all of them. No, I'm not stalking you... but I see you, self-saboteur, creeping in the shadows just waiting to torch anything good or positive. Knock it off and read this book with a highlighter!

Why do you do it?

☞ *Mommy didn't love you enough so you think you're not worthy?*

→ WRONG! Your mom doesn't go to this dojo and neither does her judgment. The only opinion about you that matters is yours and you're reading this book so you must be awesome.

☞ *You feel like you're a fraud when people compliment you because Daddy said you'd never amount to anything?*

→ WRONG! We all think that we are frauds from time to time. That doesn't stop a COBRA from winning... keep reading.

☞ Your best friend in kindergarten taught you to say "I didn't want to play anyway" and you adopted it as your answer to every rejection?

→ WRONG! That's something people say to avoid hurting someone else's feelings not words to live by. COBRAs take rejection and turn it into opportunity. We will dive into this more once you admit there's a problem.

☞ *Your buddy in junior high told you that someone had a crush on you and everyone laughed so you said "I don't think that'll ever happen" and that's been your dating strategy ever since?*

→ WRONG! Predicting your own failure will become a self-fulfilling prophecy. COBRAs are careful with what we wish for, because we don't wait around to see if it comes true, we make it happen. COBRAs are rainmakers!

YOU MUST KNOW YOUR STRENGTHS AND

WEAKNESSES TO ACHIEVE SUCCESS

Self-saboteurs are notorious for busying themselves with "faux-work" and falling prey to "Thieves of Time." Do you spend excessive time and money on things that make you feel good like food, toys, and other more nefarious vices instead of working a few extra minutes on feeling good about yourself? "Feeling good" versus feeling good about yourself sounds very similar but couldn't be further apart. Not to worry, COBRAs always have a plan, keep reading, you'll have one too.

Glad you're still with me in the dojo. You made the right choice my friend. Time to dig deeper. Ready for another quiz? See how many of these describe you.

☐ Lack of Motivation	☐ Feeling Hopeless
☐ Procrastinator	☐ Unproductive
☐ Lack of Focus	☐ Indecisive
☐ Confused	☐ Overwhelmed
☐ Struggling	☐ Stressed Out

SPOILER ALERT Once you unleash your inner badass all of the issues you choose from the list will be addressed and corrected. So be honest with yourself because it's important to know your strengths and weaknesses in order to achieve lasting success. Later on, we will focus on your weaknesses. But for now, let's figure out if you are truly BUSY or just look that way. Yeah, I'm calling you out on your time consuming Faux-Work. Let's see how bad it is or if you deserve a stripe on your white belt.

LAZINESS INCLUDES REFUSING TO WORK AND NOT WORKING SMART

If you chose 2 or more, you may be a **time-waster** engaged in faux-work; the unimportant things you tell yourself are important. Need more convincing? Let's explore the difference between being busy and being productive. Yes, there most certainly is a difference.

Like most people, you probably juggle multiple "critical" tasks at once, like watching TV, playing Fruit Ninja or checking social media while sitting on the toilet. Again, I'm not stalking you but I see you, Time-Waster, creeping in the shadows burying any chance at success under a pile of unnecessary faux-work. You're the one everyone loves to call because you jump to every incoming request, problem, and notification (yeah, I went there social media. Social media is not a daily chore unless you get paid to check it.) Despite all those callers, you still feel lonely most of the time and where are those people when you need a hand?

COBRAs prioritize based on importance instead of convenience. In doing so you may lose followers or miss your ex's new life update, but you will meet deadlines like a badass which will knock out items on your to-do list like early Mike Tyson. With your work out of the way, you will have time to relax, build your own dojo and make COBRA friends. You still with me?

FOCUS CREATES QUALITY WHICH BEATS QUANTITY EVERY TIME

Close your eyes... wait read the rest first... Now imagine the word ORGANIZATION. Be honest... you immediately conjure up the image of a company or group instead of a system to keep you on track. That lack of a connection to organization is why you're not able to focus, which leads to struggling. Struggling to meet deadlines leads to being overwhelmed. Next stop: stressed-out, unproductive and easily distracted (which is fuel for faux-work); because who wouldn't want to take a break to do something mentally rewarding like faux-work? COBRAs know that organization means planning for success. Now silence your devices and keep reading.

Are you feeling exposed sweetheart? Good! It means you are a worthy student of this dojo and open to becoming a COBRA. Pop quiz, hot shot. Are you ready to earn some dojo points? Take this quiz, you get 1 point for answering yes and 2 points for answering no. There are no wrong answers, so be honest. Total your score after you finish.

☐ yes	☐ no	Are you shy or lonely?
☐ yes	☐ no	Are you unhappy?
☐ yes	☐ no	Are you afraid?
☐ yes	☐ no	Do you feel helpless?
☐ yes	☐ no	Do you feel like you can't change?
☐ yes	☐ no	Do you feel misunderstood?

YELLOW BELT

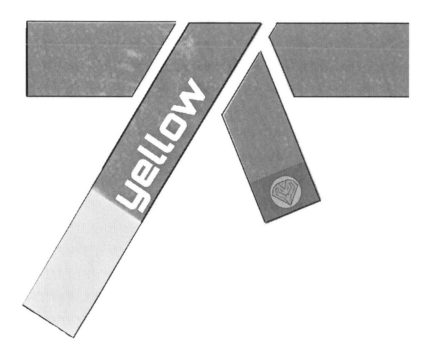

THE WAY OF THE COBRA

"From one thing, know ten thousand things. When you attain the Way of strategy there will not be one thing you cannot see. You must study hard."

-Miyamoto Musashi,
The Book of Five Rings

FIVE-CORE PILLARS

CHARACTER

OPTIMIZATION

BALANCE

RESPECT

ABUNDANCE

COBRA represents the acronym formed by the five core pillars defining the *WAY OF THE COBRA*. A COBRA embodies the spirit of each principle that together comprise the *WAY OF THE COBRA*. A COBRA is a badass, living life as the best version of himself or herself. Follow this path and it's guiding principles and it will reward you with happiness and success.

19

CHARACTER

"WATCH YOUR THOUGHTS, THEY
BECOME YOUR WORDS; WATCH
YOUR WORDS, THEY BECOME YOUR
ACTIONS; WATCH YOUR ACTIONS,
THEY BECOME YOUR HABITS;
WATCH YOUR HABITS, THEY BECOME
YOUR CHARACTER; WATCH YOUR
CHARACTER, IT BECOMES YOUR
DESTINY."

- LAO TZU

Character is what you know to be true of yourself. Character is who you are at your core and what you do when no one is watching. Character is how you treat others when you stand to gain nothing; how you go out of your way to help someone just because it's the right thing to do. Lastly, your character is the defining essence of who you are deep within when the chips are down and others panic. Guard your character with your life because your life depends upon it remaining intact. Remember these words. CHARACTER is everything. We are COBRAs, it's not enough to have character you must maintain good character.

Here are the COBRA traits of good character :

☐ Trustworthy	☐ Courageous
☐ Respectful	☐ Patient
☐ Responsible	☐ Tolerant
☐ Loyal	☐ Humble
☐ Fair	☐ Empathetic
☐ Honest	☐ Kind

A COBRA recognizes that strong character and self-knowledge create the foundation for everything else. The more you know yourself and the clearer you are about your fundamental essence, your true character, the more powerful you become. Self knowledge is a formidable ally.

COBRAs are human. Part of being human includes struggling with flaws, personal challenges, demons and repetitive obstacles. Character is not always strongest in those individuals who have lived a pristine life but rather in those who recognize their shortcomings and consistently strive to overcome them.

We've all heard the often misinterpreted cliché: "Don't worry what people think of you, it's beyond your control." That doesn't mean you should ignore how the world sees you, rather it's a warning not to **worry**. Instead take action and be the person that makes you happy without allowing outsiders' opinions to hurt your feelings. Use their opinions as a tool to decide whether you want to make a change or not.

Reputation is the raw material with which others construct their opinion of you. It's what they think of you and in turn say about you. Reputation largely determines how others treat you. Reputation is important and can take a lifetime to build only to collapse in moments. It's not fair but it's a fact. Trust me, I speak from experience. Guard your reputation like a prized treasure. Oscar Wilde said it best,

"ONLY A FOOL DOESN'T JUDGE A BOOK BY IT'S COVER."

- COBRAs do what they say and say what they mean. A COBRA's word is golden, you can take it to the bank. They don't over promise yet deliver more than expected.

- COBRAs act with integrity and honesty, not only when it is easy or being watched, but always.

- COBRAs acknowledge each person's basic worth and value. They treat everyone with dignity and respect, not for personal gain or to appear noble, but because it is the right thing to do.

- COBRAs listen to the opinions of others, especially when they conflict with your own. Contradictory arguments challenge your point of view by allowing you to consider alternative possibilities.

- A COBRA takes credit when appropriate but never minimizes the contributions of others or seeks to take undo credit.

- A COBRA avoids gossip, teasing and other unCOBRA like behavior.

- A COBRA doesn't engage in unsubstantiated rumors or traffic in negative informational currency.

- A COBRA does not speak about others with malice especially if they are not present to defend themselves.

- A COBRA doesn't ridicule or chide others under the guise of humor in an attempt to humiliate or embarrass them especially in front of others.

- A COBRA recognizes that you never know what private war another person may be fighting. Have empathy for every person's life situation.

OPTIMIZATION

PRIORITIZE OR EVERYTHING WILL
BE AN EMERGENCY. MAKE CHOICES
CAREFULLY BUT SWIFTLY THEN ACT
WITH AUDACITY.

A COBRA doesn't whine or complain about what could or should be, rather deals with what is. This requires flexibility and adaptability. COBRAs maximize their odds of success by examining available options and acting upon the optimal solution. Optimal doesn't mean perfect, it means the best solution available at the moment when you must act. Most times in life, the optimal solution executed with appropriate intensity, commitment and dedication will achieve success. In the event that isn't enough to succeed it will most likely mitigate the downside and avoid complete failure. Life's greatest opportunities and most difficult challenges, as well as, day-to-day existence never unfold at the perfect time, in the perfect place, nor under the perfect set of circumstances. Later in this book you will come to learn that perfection is a myth.

"IT IS NOT THE STRONGEST OF THE
SPECIES THAT SURVIVES, NOR THE MOST
INTELLIGENT. IT IS THE ONE THAT IS
MOST ADAPTABLE TO CHANGE."
-CHARLES DARWIN

When faced with a challenge, implement these eight steps to maximize your likelihood of producing the optimal outcome:

1. Determine the desired result.

2. Examine the challenge from all angles.

3. List the possible options for action(s) to realize success.

4. Evaluate each option (course of action).

5. Select the OPTIMAL option.

6. Anticipate potential obstacles.

7. Formulate a plan B and Plan C for contingencies

8. Act without hesitation and with audacity.

Optimize your organization.

Are you so busy that you don't have time to sit down for five minutes? No one is that busy. Do I need to send you back to "Who Needs This Book?" for a refresher in time-wasters and faux-work? The truth is that you're just not organized. Instead of running around frantically, you need a solid organization strategy. Find what works best for you, I recommend the following:

- Create a simple to-do-list with no more than three "most important tasks" (MITs). Use a to-do-list app to organize and share your lists.

- Automate recurring tasks like bill pay, mail order pharmacy, and paperless statements.

- Think like a COBRA but take note of the S.E.A.L. Not the cute little guys we root for during shark week, but the baddest warriors on the face of the planet, the U.S. Navy S.E.A.L.s. How does a S.E.A.L. eat an elephant? One bite at a time. So break down your large tasks into manageable chunks.

KNOWLEDGE IS POWER.
ESPECIALLY WHEN APPLIED CORRECTLY

Next time you're wolfing down a pizza, take a second to consider the chef's organizational system called *"mise en place."* Their process is to arrange all of the ingredients and tools before cooking. This prep-work saves time, prevents looking for misplaced items, and helps them stay on task. It's super helpful when your dojo is full of little white belts with short attention spans.

BALANCE

"WHEN WE CREATE PEACE, HARMONY
AND BALANCE IN OUR MINDS WE
WILL HAVE IT IN OUR LIVES".
- UNKNOWN

A balanced life facilitates happiness and expedites success. Achieving certain goals takes time and maintaining important relationships requires effort. Sometimes life gets in the way. At times, one area of your life demands more maintenance, attention or work than another. Other times, life has different plans for us than the ones we make for ourselves requiring a detour or pause along the journey. This happens frequently when you're trying to achieve specific goals, especially if they're punctuated with a deadline. For example, if you want a house before the age of thirty, you may have to make sacrifices depending on your financials. You may have to forgo luxuries or work a full-time job, which diminishes your leisure time. Lack of free time can create a potential strain on your relationships.

While this represents a temporary imbalance, it's a calculated risk and meant to achieve a goal that will hopefully bring you much greater happiness. Once you've reached the goal you can readjust back to a greater sense of balance by reducing the amount of time you're working. Life is a series of compromises and trade-offs. What good is fabulous wealth if you must work constantly to the exclusion of your loved ones? In time, those relationships suffer and eventually wither. Conversely not possessing the financial means to provide for and protect your loved ones creates insecurity, chaos and resentment.

Too much eating and not enough exercise results in a physical imbalance manifesting in excessive body weight. Too much self denial and rigid disciple can result in a confining and limited life and lead to unhappiness. Creating a balanced life is tricky and in truth, a bit of an art form. Everyone's life is messy.

- Accept that achieving balance is a process that won't happen over night nor without trial and error.

- Balance requires self awareness which

develops over time and through experience.

- Decide who and what in your life is truly important.

- Minimize or eliminate who and what does not enhance your balance.

"YOU CAN'T HAVE EVERYTHING AND DO EVERYTHING AT THE SAME TIME."
- OPRAH

Stress is the biggest culprit in the loss of balance. Stress can manifest in ways that are obvious, like anxiety, moodiness, and tension. But it's sinister reach is far beyond the obvious. Stress can make you gain weight, by interfering with your cortisol levels and by the comfort food you eat to tame the stress beast. Stress can cause aches and pains and even trick your body into becoming sick or at least thinking it is, like panic attacks that masquerade as heart attacks. Don't neglect stress management because unlike a cobra, you can not regenerate your lost appendages.

If your stress becomes overwhelming it's time to HALT. It stands for Hungry Angry Lonely Tired, all feelings that are by-products of stress. So if you're experiencing any of these, ask yourself: is it stress induced or are you truly in need of action? Sometimes addressing one of these four issues alleviates the overall feeling of stress which allows you to return to balance. So, have a snack, phone a friend, or take a nap.

RESPECT

"RESPECT YOURSELF AND OTHERS
WILL RESPECT YOU."

- CONFUCIUS

The simplest and most profound advice about respect comes from the COBRA's golden rule: "Do unto others as you would have them do unto you." This simple concept appears in almost every major religion and culture in some form or another because respect forms the foundation for every relationship. Well, at least, every successful relationship where respect is earned, not given. Successful relationships require both members to earn each others trust by maintaining mutual respect. A COBRA keeps their side of the street clean which clears the way for respect to be returned, even in the most difficult of times. You can love someone and if the relationship is not built upon mutual respect it will fail.

Before expecting respect from others you must respect yourself. Define your rulebook, ask yourself what you will and will not tolerate from yourself because respect begins with you. People largely decide how they will treat you by the way they see you treat yourself. You must train others how to treat you, so be good to yourself or no one else will.

Now more than ever respect is critically important to success. Much of our society has lost the ability to behave with civility and common courtesy. Respect must start at home, especially if you have children. In doing so, you bring respect into the world on a grassroots level which permeates school, work and the world at large.

We've all heard a story about the exceedingly gifted athlete who simply cannot conform to the rules and codes of ethics and respect that unify a team. On field success only protects a player temporarily. Once his or her lack of respect comes to the attention of colleagues and superiors it will be treated like a cancer. It must be cut out so it doesn't infect the rest of the team. You can possess all the innate talent in the world but if you do not demonstrate respect to your co-workers and superiors you will fail. They will make sure of it. Sooner or later a lack of respect even in the most talented individuals will result in their downfall.

GRATITUDE FUELS FAITH.
FAITH CONTROLS DESTINY.

-MICHELE KANAN

The one thing a COBRA does not respect is the status quo, not in themselves, their relationships or business. If you are not constantly seeking to improve, you stagnate and will eventually erode. Every day and in every way you must make a continued effort to improve EVERYTHING. What worked yesterday may not work tomorrow. Remember fax machines? Stores on every corner that offered facsimile services. They have now gone the way of the dinosaur. Maintaining success proves much more difficult than achieving it in the first place.

Now, I'm no rocket scientist. Hell, I didn't even take physics in high school. However, I do know the second law of thermodynamics: entropy. This law basically states that all systems move towards disorder and deterioration. While this may be a law of the universe, you can do your level best to fight against it. The best way is to stay in motion. I don't know if it's a law of the universe but I've certainly found this to be true for me: Keep moving, keep grinding and keep learning. Continued work towards improvement gets results. Taking even small actions over time can yield big results. Do not fall under the illusion that past success in any way ensures future success. Constantly look to disrupt the status quo in yourself, your relationships, and your business. By disrupt I mean consistently working to find new and better ways to bring value to each of these areas. Remember, that the COBRA who rests on his or her laurels stands up with thorns in their tail.

My 50th birthday was one of the most incredible days of my life. Not one of the most incredible birthdays but one of the most incredible days and I've been blessed to have had some pretty darn spectacular ones. As a surprise, my wife, Michele, organized for me to be honored with a star on the Palm Springs Walk of Fame to commemorate my career and contribution to the Arts. She secretly arranged for my family to fly in, for a wide array of my friends to attend the unveiling of the star and for the mayor to present me with a proclamation signed by our state senator deeming the day "Sean Kanan Day". Several people very meaningful in my life, including my old Karate Kid III amigo, Martin Kove (aka Sensei John Kreese) spoke at the ceremony. I was blown away. The ability for an author to express themselves in a book is, well, kind of important and yet I cannot adequately convey the myriad of emotions I felt that day; which were compounded later that evening. The surprises continued with an amazing party in a very swanky home. To say I let my hair down would be a tad understated. A celebration, which lasted five days, including a constant parade of guests spanning my entire life and spectrum of friends. It was like a recap of my entire existence in one week.

When the dust settled and the smoke cleared it was time to get back to reality. But in the weeks and months to follow I began to sink into a funk. Not a full-blown depression but rather a confusing period of conflicting emotions. It was more than just the come down from such an emotional high, I felt stuck. I was stagnating, trapped in the quicksand of inertia which is defined as the tendency to do nothing or to remain unchanged. Unfortunately this wasn't completely uncharted territory. Once again I felt like a fraud, here I had just been honored for my accomplishments and success and I didn't have a damn clue what to do next. If I'm being completely honest, which is what a Sensei always is with his students, I was flat out scared. Fear can be quite a motivator, so I pulled up my COBRA pants and consulted my mentors.

With the clarity gained by looking through the prism of my mentors and a pep-talk from my wife, I realized I was in desperate need of reinventing myself... at 50. Although it was a motivating win to identify the problem, the solution seemed to terrify me. I knew to have any possibility of achieving a complete "re-brand" would require a disruption of the status quo in my life, in the way I viewed myself and the world around me, again. But this time I didn't have the youth factor as a safety net. I would be forced to get honest and really deconstruct what made me tick with the added pressure of possibly disappointing my wife and possibly coming to the conclusion that I was ...old... irrelevant... done. But, this is what sets COBRAs apart, we do the tough work, we persevere. I started with a list of what I currently enjoyed doing and assigned a reason why I enjoyed it. During this process of introspection I stumbled upon some realizations.

One of the most significant ones involved my career as an actor. As long as I can remember I wanted to be an actor, it has been who I am and what has defined me. I love acting. When I first started formulating the idea of becoming an actor, much of it came from a fifteen year old boy's desire to express himself and be seen by the world. As the years passed and I matured as both an actor and a man, I clarified that the core reason why I wanted to become an actor wasn't to express myself, although that's part of it, but rather to inspire the world. But it went further and deeper, I wanted to make a difference in peoples lives. I came to realize that acting wasn't the only way I could accomplish this. I took an inventory of events outside of acting that have allowed me to inspire people. I lobbied in Congress against bullying, delivered a keynote speech at a benefit for Autism Research, and traveled with the USO to Bosnia and Kosovo to entertain the troops. I had discovered the most significant WHY in my life next to my marriage, inspiring others. This initiated a new phase in my life.

I could tell you that it all came together like mom's cooking in a New York minute but I'd be lying. There were speed bumps. There were setbacks. There were false starts. And guess what? There still are. Not as many or as frequent, but they are a part of life for all of us. But for me, my second act includes sharing my success through writing, coaching and motivational speaking. If you struggle with feelings of stuck-ness, STAY IN THE STRUGGLE. Keep fighting to disrupt the status quo in your life and you can make a monumental shift in your life. Know that it's a process and therefore takes time but also know that you are on the right path. Know that I am with you. You are a part of this dojo and are not alone. If I can do it you can do it. Remember, transform yourself and you can transform the world.

ABUNDANCE

"WHEN YOU REALIZE THERE IS
NOTHING LACKING, THE WHOLE
WORLD BELONGS TO YOU."

- LAO TZU

Living in abundance is simple yet humans make it so difficult because of fear; fear of not having enough. Fear of having someone or something taken away. Fear that abundance may not exist. A perpetual state of gratitude ensures that you live in abundance. COBRAs recognize that the universe holds an infinite amount of success, wealth, love and happiness for everyone. No one else's life of abundance diminishes the possibility of your life of abundance. Abundance and love share the similarity that the more you hold onto it, the less you will have. The fastest way to increase either one is to give it away. Think of it like a candle, it can be used to light other candles without diminishing the flame. The more candles you light, the brighter your world will become.

Sharing your good fortune and experience with others increases your circle of friends and positive energy. The more you do this the more positive energy you create. This energy is boundless and surrounds you with abundance. A COBRA lives an existence of endless possibilities recognizing only they can limit themselves by mindset and words. Thoughts are things. The images, stories and associations we create either limit or increase our abundance.

A COBRA chooses words carefully never creating or reinforcing an atmosphere of scarcity or victimhood but rather abundance and empowerment. Language has a tremendous influence on our reality. Conversely, take care not to allow the careless or poorly chosen words of others to negatively affect your reality. Remember, words have consequences. I employ a little saying "THINK before you speak." T= is it truthful? H= is it helpful? I= is it inspiring? N= is it necessary? K= is it kind?

WIN-WIN vs ZERO SUM GAME

This concept represents the nexus between respect and abundance. There are very few times in life that present a zero-sum game; meaning you have to lose for me to win. An infinitely more desirable strategy is the win-win. This requires respect for the other party and the acknowledgment that compromise is not a loss, rather it's an opportunity to move forward while only sacrificing a small amount. In the long run, by giving a little, you avoid conflict, negativity, and stalemate. Remember you live in a world of abundance, where almost without exception, exists the possibility for you to win. In the process, you can help others realize their goals too. When you come from a place of abundance, not scarcity, anything is possible whether in business or interpersonal relationships. Anyone can best the opposition once, COBRAs build a relationship by achieving their goals in tandem with others.

☐ Live in a state of gratitude.

☐ Cultivate optimism.

☐ Learn to live with less even while striving for more.

☐ Know that the universe wants you to succeed.

☐ Take care not to define abundance only by possessions and money.

☐ Recognize that life has improved significantly across the ages.

☐ Give in abundance to live in abundance. This doesn't necessarily mean money. You can give time, kindness and emotional connection.

ORANGE BELT

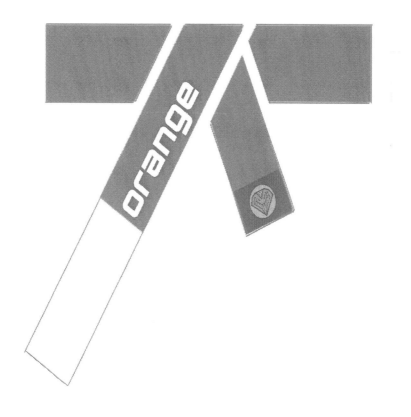

WE SHALL SEE

Release yourself from the worry about what may happen; live in the present.

A COBRA knows emotions are based upon perception of circumstance and that perception frequently changes as new information emerges.

Christmas Day 1988. While the rest of the world celebrated with family and friends, I found myself in an emergency room at Sunrise Hospital in Las Vegas, bleeding to death. I was 22 years old. How I got there is a great story. What I learned from the experience has proven a life-altering lesson. Let's go back a few months before that fateful day.

I stared in sheer disbelief. "So many", I thought to myself. The open call attracted more hopefuls than I had anticipated. Way more. The line stretched around the outside of Columbia Studios in Burbank that warm autumn morning. Exactly why I had shown up unannounced the day before at the office of the casting director for The Karate Kid III. The studio was searching for the newest member of the Cobra Kai, "Mike Barnes", "Karate's Bad Boy", described as a seventeen-year-old white Mike Tyson terrorizing Daniel LaRusso. The role, one of the most sought after parts in all of Hollywood at the time, represented a huge break for any actor fortunate enough to win the job. I had already decided that actor was going to be me. Pretty damn cocky for a young kid from a small town in Western Pennsylvania. Especially considering that only a few years before I was just another paying customer in the theater watching Mr. Miyagi imparting words of wisdom to Daniel-san.

Now, without an appointment, I finagled my way into the casting director's office hoping to circumvent the cattle call. Young and naïve I assumed the casting director would appreciate seeing me. After all, I had my Screen Actors Guild card and had appeared in one episode of a soon-to-be-canceled, primetime, television show. I was a "real" actor. I explained that my martial arts teacher, Master Fumio Demura, served as Pat Morita's stunt double. It was Master Demura who first told me about the open call. I trained in Japanese karate since I was thirteen years old. The role was made for me and I was going to do everything humanly possible to win the part but first I had to impress the casting director, Caro Jones.

Unfortunately, that afternoon "me and Mrs. Jones did not have a thing going on". (It's an old song. Google it.) She refused to allow me to read for her and concluded our brief encounter by informing me that I was free to fight it out at the open call like everyone else. I was dejected but not deterred. COBRAs do not take "No" for an answer.

The next day at the open call I took my place in the seemingly endless line after being handed a piece of paper with a number on it to identify me. Later I would learn that they were well over 1500 young men standing in front of the studio that day. They all had one thing in common. They wanted my job and that was not going to happen.

However in order to move closer to winning the role I would have to capture the attention of one individual in particular, John Avildsen. The diminutive director served at the helm of the first two Karate Kid films. He also won an Oscar in 1976 for directing the story of another underdog fighting against the odds by the name of Rocky Balboa. Avildsen and his entourage moved swiftly but thoughtfully from the back of the line towards the front. He carried a small video recorder occasionally filming those candidates he deemed interesting. I knew I would have only a few fleeting seconds to try and engage him. We locked eyes and he stopped before me. This was it. It would all come down to the next few seconds. Generally success occurs over a period of time filled with hard work, persistence and dedication. This was not one of those times. Some moments that define our lives unfold in an instant. This was one of those moments.

The director quickly explained that we were going to do a quick improvisation in which I should intimidate him. My mind raced for a few split seconds before settling upon the words to use. I don't member exactly what I said but I do recall that it had something to do with a butcher's knife and paying Mr. Avildsen a visit in his kitchen later that evening if he didn't give me a screen test. A long silence followed. Had I gone too far? Did this older gentleman almost half a foot shorter than me think I was a psycho? Apparently he did which turned out to be a good thing. "I buy it" he said to an assistant who glanced at my number and notated it on a clipboard before pulling me out of line. I was quickly ushered into the studio. I had done it! I successfully cleared the first hurdle. After a few moments I found myself inside a massive soundstage the size of an airplane hangar.

If the chaos outside seemed daunting, this was a regular circus. Press crews filmed behind the scenes - Entertainment Tonight, Access Hollywood to name just a few. I looked around trying to absorb as much information as possible. I quickly calculated there were ten other young guys who had been brought inside the competition.

Suddenly a young lady took my hand and pulled me towards a nearby chair. She quickly applied some makeup on my face, while I was unable to conceal my overwhelmed expression. Next I was brought to a set erected specifically for the screen test. Several yards away from me stood Ralph Macchio, already a big star thanks to the success of the first two Karate Kid films and his earlier role in "The Outsiders" alongside Patrick Swayze, Matt Dillon and Tom Cruise. Ironically, I would later star in the short lived Fox television series "The Outsiders" based on the film and the original book by S.E. Hinton.

I knew if I looked at this guy like a big Hollywood actor I would blow it. I had to focus. I was there for one reason only, to scare the shit out of a guy I'd watched many times before in the theater. I was face-to-face with THE Karate kid. The director gave me one simple command. Intimidate him. A bell rang indicating all noise and work needed to stop. The director called "Action". It was go time. Ralph barely uttered a line when I exploded into a front stance throwing a downward block while snarling with a loud, guttural kiai. I moved aggressively, backing him into a corner. He must've thought I was unhinged because he started yelling "Call him off, call him off." After a tense second or two Ralph began to smile. Apparently I was convincing. I broke into a smile. After all he was the star and I didn't want him to think I was really crazy. I noticed some of the producers whispering back-and-forth while looking at me. I felt good. Hell, I felt damn good. I was then asked to film a quick interview with Entertainment Tonight. Entertainment tonight! Everything seemed surreal yet empowering.

I tore out of the studio parking lot in my red Mustang. I made my way down the Sunset Strip past the jungle of billboards advertising movie stars and their latest films. After a few more minutes I arrived at my unremarkable one-bedroom apartment above the world famous Whiskey-a-GoGo. My head swimming, I couldn't help but feel I had a shot, a good shot at winning the role.

Several days later I learned the devastating truth. The role, my role, had gone to someone else. I was devastated. Until that moment I don't think I'd ever experienced such soul-crushing unhappiness. In a relatively short time I would learn what real unhappiness felt like. But first fate had another incredible surprise in store for me. A week after filming began the decision was made to fire the actor chosen to play Mike Barnes and I received a call from the film's executive producer, Sheldon Schrager asking me to come to his office on the lot at Columbia Pictures.

I could barely contain my excitement as I drove to the studio. Off in the distance loomed the iconic Hollywood sign. Actors have a saying, "Sometimes the Hollywood sign smiles at you and other times it smirks." It was definitely smiling at me that day. Once at the office I was greeted by Mr. Schrager and writer Robert Mark Kamen, who created The Karate Kid and would later go on to write blockbusters such as Taken and The Transporter. Kamen, a black belt himself, asked me to perform a few simple karate techniques which I easily executed. He and the producer appeared satisfied. They went into an adjoining room with some other members of the production staff. I waited outside nervously anticipating the decision. Mr. Schrager reemerged a few moments later and proceeded to tell me that I was hired. Just like that I joined the cast of one of the most well-known franchises in the world. I felt an incredible sense of elation. As much as I wanted to call my parents and my friends there simply wasn't any time. I was immediately brought to wardrobe and proceeded to meet many of the key people on the production. I didn't return home that day until well after dark. I remember the lights on the Sunset Strip had a strange, warm glow that evening seeming somehow friendlier than just a night before. I could hardly believe the miraculous turn of events that had occurred in the last 24 hours of my young life.

I landed on the floor of the Cobra Kai dojo with a resounding thud. I'd lost count how many times I had thrown myself to the ground so that we could get the shot just right. It was a simple action requiring me to jump a few feet and then fall to the ground landing on my side. The director patiently explained to me earlier in the day that the editor would pair that shot with another one where I come flying through the door courtesy of Mr. Miyagi. Later when the scene was pieced together it would look quite convincing. The assistant director yelled "cut" then"checking the gate".

After several weeks of filming I began to acquire a whole new vocabulary used in filmmaking. "Checking the gate" refers to the moment after a take when the cameraman checks the gate of *the camera where the film passes in front of the lens making sure that no dust or hair are present that could damage the film. It also meant that if the first A.D. (assistant director) yelled a subsequent word then production would officially break for the Christmas holiday. After a tense few seconds "Print" rang out across the set as the actors and crew cheered. Everyone began shaking hands and saying goodbye. We were all looking forward to a well-deserved break. The filming had been extremely physical and exhausting for everyone, especially the actors who underwent intense martial arts training in conjunction with learning a tremendous amount of fight choreography. I was constantly sore during filming. As I walked off set toward my modest trailer, I became acutely aware of a dull persistent aching in my upper left thigh. I assumed it was an occupational hazard from the training. I couldn't wait to ice it down and take some aspirin. I was looking forward to a trip to Vegas for the holidays with my friend.*

I sat in the passenger seat while she drove her black Wrangler Jeep across the desert. The roof was down and the warm night air was intoxicating. I stared up at the stars and pondered the moment taking stock of my life. I was 22 years old and living my dream. A dream that began outside a gas station in a small town in Western Pennsylvania where I confided to my friends that I was going to win the role as the new heavy in The Karate Kid III. As the Jeep climbed the ridge just before hitting Vegas I got the familiar feeling of excitement in my gut as the lights bathed my face. The kaleidoscope of colors reached out to me like my future. After a moment I snapped back to reality. That nagging pain in my leg had grown more persistent which meant another handful of aspirin. Although I had been throwing martial arts kicks on a daily basis for weeks this pain seemed different. I was about to learn just how different.

Christmas Eve in Sin City. Standing in the middle of the old Dunes casino I looked across the sea of green felt gaming tables in search of an answer as to what I was experiencing. A few moments ago I was having fun deciding where to lose my money next. Suddenly I felt my blood pressure dropping and I became dizzy and confused. A questioning expression filled my face. I collapsed to the ground and fell unconscious. Security guards and paramedics knelt over me while I was still on the floor. They loaded me onto a stretcher and then hurried me into a nearby ambulance that raced away from the hotel to Humana Sunrise Hospital. I overheard one of the paramedics say that I passed out because my blood pressure had plummeted due to extreme loss of blood. I'll never forget the next words I heard: "Let's get him to the ER, he's dying." What came next was a blur with the exception of a few key moments. I was in an observation room in the ER. A nurse gently but intensely explained that I required an operation to stop the bleeding. I was now suffering from acute abdominal pain. The nurse told me they were going to operate immediately. She handed me a release form to sign acknowledging I understood the hospital could not guarantee my life would be saved. I had perforated my greater omentum which sits on top of the intestine. I'd never even heard of a greater omentum but apparently mine had been bleeding internally for days. The pain in my left thigh was a result of blood dripping on my femoral artery. The constant battery of aspirin I'd been swallowing exacerbated the bleeding. I couldn't believe this was happening.

The nurse looked at me with genuine compassion in her eyes. She reassured me or at least tried saying that I was young and strong but I would have to fight. At that point things began to get very real very quickly. I was no longer fighting to win a role in a film. I was involved in the fight for my life. The pain intensified. I grew colder and colder struggling to keep my eyes open. I felt myself starting to slip away. I remember thinking how easy it would be to just let go and drift off to sleep. I forced myself to stay focused and alert as I was wheeled into the operating room.

All the while imagining my parents reaction to being awakened at midnight back in Pennsylvania with the news their son was in emergency surgery. The operating room buzzed with activity as the emergency surgery team prepped for the operation. Two figures dressed in scrubs hovered above me. I presumed the one about to place a mask over my face was the anesthesiologist and the other one was the surgeon. I looked the surgeon in the eyes and summoned what little strength I had left and said, " Tell me that you're good." From behind his mask he spoke with a foreign accent "Don't worry, don't worry." I repeated the words again this time with all the strength and conviction I had. "Tell me… that… you're good." My eyes pleaded for some reassurance. The doctor pulled down his mask just slightly and smiled. "I'm good." The mask descended onto my face as I counted backward, " Ten, nine, ei...ght...".

I woke up in a hospital room. I had survived and had an angry 12 inch vertical incision along my abdomen to prove it. The wound was lined with giant staples sticking out of my flesh. The anesthesia had worn off as well as the painkillers, and I hurt like hell. Another patient rested in the bed next to me. He would later die. My father sat in a chair across from me. It was obvious he hadn't slept. My parents were only able to find one ticket on such short notice. They decided my father would leave immediately and my mom would follow on the next available flight. I can't imagine the fear and feeling of powerlessness that must've tormented my father during that flight.

The first thing, the only thing on my mind was saving my role in the film. My mind raced as I contemplated how this would play out. I didn't need to guess for too long. The phone rang. It was the director, John Avildsen. After a terse "How you doing" he informed me that I would have approximately a week or so to return to production. If by some miracle of human physiology I did manage to return to set in time they we would use a stunt man to perform all of my martial arts sequences. If I could not return then I would be replaced. I would later learn that most likely it would've been Bruce Lee's son Brandon Lee who would replace me.

No flowers filled my room. No card wishing me a speedy recovery from the studio, just a cold and insensitive objectivity from the production. I hung up the phone and could barely speak. I thought to myself, "Welcome to Hollywood kid". The pain at that moment was infinitely more cutting than when I learned I did not get the part. You know that line in the song "A taste of honey is worse than none at all?" That's bullshit. I was certain I was experiencing the most profound unhappiness of my life. At one point I told my father that if I couldn't finish the film, I didn't want to live. In retrospect that may have been a little dramatic but what do you want? I'm an actor.

Then something interesting began to take root deep within me. I was getting mad. I burned with determination fueled by anger from the injustice visited upon me. I'd come too damn far to let the chance of a lifetime slip through my fingers. I decided right then and there to leave my hospital bed and start the daunting task of rehabilitating myself. My bare feet touched the cold floor. I stood up wearing only my hospital gown. I couldn't believe how weak I felt. I'd lost a tremendous amount of weight in a very short time. The weight loss combined with my new flat top haircut gave me the ghostly appearance of a malnourished prisoner of war. My abdomen seared with pain from the large postoperative wound. I smiled faintly at my dad and I started to walk – first one foot than the other. I managed to fight through the pain and walk the entire *hospital floor that first day. The next day I walked farther and farther the next. I don't remember how many days I stayed in the hospital, but I had myself released against medical advice. I was determined to make it back to the set and determined to finish the film.*

Back at production, the decision was made to use the stunt man for the martial arts choreography and use me for the close-ups. This was far from ideal but at least for the moment it appeared "The kid stays in the picture. (The Sun Also Rises, Robert Evans, Google it.) The production enlisted the services of Dan Isaacson, a celebrity trainer and ex-Los Angeles Ram's lineman, Kyle Borland, to oversee my recovery. Each day I pushed myself harder and harder to get back in condition. I hadn't realized how weak I had become and how much the surgery had taken out of me. Slowly, I began gaining back some muscle. I was getting stronger. I went from a handful of sit ups each workout to doing hundreds. Eventually, after watching me perform the various martial arts sequences, the producers were convinced and agreed to let me resume full responsibility for my role. With the exception of one driving stunt I executed every single one of my characters' martial arts moves and fight stunts in the film.

To this day I'm extremely proud of the fact that I battled my way back in time to do all my own stunts. Cobras are always their most dangerous when backed into a corner. Looking back on the entire experience I realize that it was one of the most defining events of my life. The universe tested me and I not only survived but overcame.

By succeeding, you reveal part of your character, the very foundation of WAY OF THE COBRA. Character is what you do when no one is watching. Character is how you react to life's challenges and disappointments. Character is how you treat others. Character determines much of your life. A true COBRA knows that it must be protected, nurtured and constantly refined. What seemed at the moment like the lowest point of my life proved in the end to help mold me as a man. It still remains one of the most important lessons that I've ever learned. I would not change any part of that chapter of my life.

THE STEEL OF OUR CHARACTER IS FORGED
FROM THE FIRES OF ADVERSITY.

Who we are is determined by how we respond to life's

challenges. Everyone one of us has faced and will keep facing life's difficulties. No one of us escapes this stark reality. Ultimately, We are defined and remembered by how we battle these obstacles and how they change us.

Two people can encounter the same experience with dramatically different outcomes. How they choose to process it and the ending they choose to attach to the story make all the difference. Only time reveals if the experience proves to have a "positive" or "negative" effect. What we perceive as "positive" in one moment in time may very possibly prove "negative" down the road and vice versa. Two young boys each grow up with an abusive, alcoholic father. Upon reaching adulthood the first child sinks into alcoholism and inflicts chaos and violence upon his family. The second child attaches a very different story to his experience. He vows to never consume alcohol and shows his family selfless love refusing to reproduce the painful experience he himself endured. In hindsight the second child grew up recognizing his painful childhood as a catalyst which molded him into a loving and empathetic adult. The experience which was initially classified as "negative" has now become "positive" over the passage of time with the attachment of a different story.

As time expands we often realize that our initial beliefs and feelings could not be farther from the truth. One way that we can minimize life's natural suffering is to regulate the emotional attachment we assign to any event. This requires *emotional discipline*. Those moments in our lives that we categorize as "bad' are rarely as "bad" as we perceive them to be. Conversely those moments of pleasure are fleeting and therefore rarely last. To put it simply "into each life some rain shall fall," and on the flip-side "tomorrow's another day." Life experiences that we emotionally categorized as "painful, horrible and destructive" frequently prove to serve as our most effective teachers. We then reassign different adjectives like "invaluable", "life-changing" and "evolutionary". This is certainly the case for me regarding the emotional roller coaster I endured during the audition process and filming of *The Karate Kid III*.

The very moment I learned I was not getting the role of Mike Barnes I created a barrage of negative associations. Just a short time later I received new positive information creating feelings of euphoria. Would I have experienced the new, "positive" information with the same emotional attachment had I known what was in store for me? Within weeks my injury drove me to the depths of despair. Once again my reality shifted 180°. By willing myself back to health and rejoining the production I was able to finish the film which propelled me to a new emotional high. And on it goes.

> "THE SECRET OF CHANGE IS TO FOCUS ALL OF YOUR ENERGY NOT ON FIGHTING THE OLD, BUT ON BUILDING THE NEW."
>
> -SOCRATES

Here's an example of emotional self-discipline properly applied. Maintaining composure and objectivity in the face of challenges allows for positive outcomes. The protagonist in the following story was indeed a King COBRA.

Many centuries ago there lived an old Chinese farmer known throughout his province as a man of wisdom. He owned a modest farm with his only son. One morning their only horse escaped from the corral. The Farmer's neighbor was quick to offer his condolences. "What misfortune, my friend." The old farmer simply replied "We shall see." Several days passed when the horse returned with a band of wild mustangs. "What great fortune," exclaimed the farmer's neighbor, "Now you may clear your field in a fraction of the time." The farmer simply replied "We shall see." The next day the old farmer's son entered the corral to saddle one of the mustangs to be used for chores. He tried valiantly to mount one of the bucking mustangs, finally succeeding but was soon thrown viciously to the ground, shattering his leg; a serious injury in those days. The neighbor lamented "What bad fortune, my friend." The farmer simply replied "We shall see." The next day the regional warlord and 100 of his soldiers appeared at the old farmer's farm. They were riding from farm to farm recruiting all the young men for their army engaged in a war against a distant province. Because the old farmer's son had been injured from the fall, he was unable to join the army. The neighbor, relieved for his friend, declared "What good fortune." The old farmer smiled and simply replied once again "We shall see." And on it goes ad infinitum.

What often initially appears as a challenge may, with the passage of time, prove to be a benefit. Resist the temptation to immediately assign a negative story to an event or situation. Heed the advice of the wise farmer. Watch how things unfold and remember, "We shall see."

BLUE BELT

INTERNAL OBSTACLES

"Success is not to be measured by the position someone has reached in life, but the obstacles he has overcome while trying to succeed."

-Booker T. Washington

Every one of us must confront obstacles. You may choose to go over, under, around or through them. You must not choose to retreat from them or they will consume you. They will stifle your creativity, your ability to connect with others and diminish your ability to impact the world. Reincarnation aside we have one shot at life. There is no dress rehearsal. It's like Apollo Creed said to Rocky. "There is no tomorrow". Your life is happening NOW in real time and make no mistake, life waits for no one. It's time to identify the obstacles that have been holding you back. They appear in two forms: external and internal obstacles. The internal, of which there are many, far and away present the bigger challenge. Which is exactly why we are going to tackle them first. Don't despair. You got this. A COBRA never shies away from a meaningful challenge offering the opportunity for self-improvement.

FEAR

"COWARDS DIE MANY TIMES BEFORE
THEIR DEATHS; THE VALIANT NEVER
TASTES OF DEATH BUT ONCE."

-WILLIAM SHAKESPEARE-

"JULIUS CAESAR"

The word fear forms the acronym from the phrase: False Evidence Appearing Real. Have you ever noticed that, not always but a significant portion of the time, our deepest fears never come to pass? How often have you wasted emotional energy or even worse, lost out on quality time with loved ones because you cooked in a stew of your own swirling fears? All because you "knew" how a specific, or even worse, a non-specific event would conclude. Ask yourself what has been standing in the way of you and the life you desire. Do you have a clear idea of what or whom that looks like? What force, real or imagined, keeps you from releasing your inner badass into the world? Let me tell you what it's not. It's not your difficult boss. It's not your disappointing kids. It's not your spouse that doesn't understand you. It's not your overbearing and constantly disappointed parents. Those are excuses. The only thing holding you back is you; more accurately your fear. Are you going to continue to allow fear to deprive you of the life you deserve?

Where does fear originate?

Fear wears many masks but originates from relatively few sources:

☐ Fear of Death	☐ Fear of Success
☐ Fear of Change	☐ Fear of Humiliation
☐ Fear of Loss of control	☐ Fear of Rejection
☐ Fear of Failure	☐ Rational Fear

1. Fear of death.

"NO ONE GETS OUT ALIVE ANYWAY."

-JIM MORRISON, THE DOORS

Condemned murder Robert Alton Harris's last words before entering the gas chamber aka "The Coughing Box"at San Quentin prison were "You can be a king or a street sweeper but everyone dances with the Grim Reaper." Pretty dead on. No pun intended. This is one of the most natural fears in the world so give yourself a break. It's human nature to fear the unknown. Consider this: you had no fear before you were born, before you existed. Why should you fear once you are gone? It is a far better existence to immerse yourself in this great adventure called life than to worry and speculate about the unknown. After all, we know how the story ends and it's the same for all of us. Why not enjoy the ride?

It's natural to worry about your health as you age or to fear a painful death. It's also common for you to worry about your friends and family after you're gone. Awareness of your mortality can be a profound challenge to your sense of well-being and your importance in the universe. It can alert you to the fragility of life, serving as a warning that you should not squander your days. COBRAs don't waste precious time worrying excessively about death. Instead they appreciate the time they are gifted, using it wisely to learn, connect, and contribute to the world, making it a better place.

"EVERY MAN DIES.NOT EVERY MAN LIVES."

-SIR WILLIAM WALLACE

There is no reason to think that the experience of temporarily losing consciousness is any different from the experience of permanently losing consciousness in terms of how the actual process feels. While some fear is healthy because it makes us more cautious, some people may also have an unhealthy, unusual or abnormal fear of dying and/or being dead that impacts the otherwise "normal" or healthy functioning of the person's daily life. When death comes for us, let it find us among the living.

2. Fear of change.

"TIME MAY CHANGE ME,

BUT I CAN'T CHANGE TIME."

- DAVID BOWIE

Generally speaking human beings are leery of change. They tend to like predictability, routine and *status quo*. It's true that those three things can provide stability and enhance safety but don't make up the whole puzzle that is a happy life. On the flipside is the ability to be a disruptor of *status quo*, willingness to take a leap of faith and initiation change. Without these, we would still be living in caves, certainly wouldn't have been to the moon or eradicated countless previously deadly illnesses. Equal measures of both is the balance necessary for a meaningful and fulfilled life.

A COBRA anticipates and welcomes change while living in the present. Which, by the way, is constantly changing into the past. Seem a bit esoteric? Allow me to simplify. Life offers no guarantees. Wherever you are now, you may not be in the future and that's ok because you will be somewhere else maybe better, maybe not. So don't waste time wondering in fear of change, **fully enjoy** your present with no attachment to whether or not you will be there in the future.

CAUTION:

"No attachment" does not mean that you don't protect what you have nor plan for the future. It simply means enjoy it while you have it instead of spending all of your time worrying it will change or be gone tomorrow.

3. Fear of Loss of Control

"I'VE LEARNED THAT WHEN YOU TRY TO CONTROL EVERYTHING, YOU ENJOY NOTHING."

-ANNE-SOPHIE VEGA

I'm gonna let you in on a little secret. Control is an illusion, it doesn't exist, more on that later in this belt. The only thing that you can control are your emotions and how you choose to react to any given situation or set of circumstances. People who believe that they are in control and are chronically afraid of losing it are often referred to as control freaks; because they "freak out" as their fears manifest. They no longer have control over their emotions and can suddenly become very angry, nervous or depressed when overwhelmed with variables.

In general, controlling people try to control others and/or situations. They may do so out of anxiety because they worry that if they do not maintain control, things will go wrong or worse, something terrible will happen to them. This fear is usually founded in trauma involving violence of some sort, whether viewed or suffered. Similarly, the control freak might not know how to form healthy relationships with others leaving them to feel like they can only depend upon themselves. Deep down, control freaks are terrified of being vulnerable and deep-down they're anxious, insecure and angry. They believe they can protect themselves by staying in control of every aspect of their lives including masking their fear with orderly obsession. Others, on the nefarious end of the control spectrum, adopt controlling behaviors to assert dominance or for personal gain, more on this later in EXTERNAL OBSTACLES. COBRAs try to control what happens in their lives to an extent, but know when to let fate take it's course and roll with the punches. They also have a backup plan for unforeseen contingencies.

You want to become a COBRA? Then push yourself to take a chance instead of demanding certainty. Resign yourself to accepting probable outcomes instead of guarantees. Focus on the fact that letting go means more freedom. Let go of control and embrace the art of surrender. When you can't control what's happening, challenge yourself to control the way you respond to what's happening, that's where you have power.

4. Fear of Failure

"I AM NOT IN COMPETITION WITH ANYONE
BUT MYSELF. MY GOAL IS TO IMPROVE
MYSELF CONTINUOUSLY."

- BILL GATES

We live in a society that is obsessed with success. It's no surprise that fear of failure is one of the most common fears that we all face. The origin comes from your childhood when you were vulnerable and in many cases inexperienced. Times when you attempted something yet didn't achieve the desired result, then suffered withering criticism from those around you, often those closest to you. Ironically, the criticism could have been unintended, but your immature brain did not have the tools to attach the correct intent at the time. That combination formed a perfect storm in your psyche, imprinting a negative story that all too often reverberates into your adult brain in the form of sweaty palms, weak knees, even a full blown panic attack. Fear of failure behaves like emotional quicksand, it keeps us not only stuck but slowly sinking into mediocrity or worse. It inhibits the desire to take chances even calculated risks.

You can dramatically reduce the anxiety that surrounds fear of failure by recognizing a few simple concepts.

- Everyone "fails" from time to time. Babe Ruth was one of the most prodigious home run hitters in the history of baseball. He also held the record for striking out more than any other player.

- Failure serves as a teacher. A reporter once asked Thomas Edison how it felt to fail 1,000 times in his quest to create the first incandescent light bulb. Edison replied, "I didn't fail 1,000 times. The light bulb was an invention with 1,000 steps. Great success is built on failure, frustration, even catastrophe."

- The only person you need to compete against is yourself. True failure only occurs when you don't try your best, learn from your mistakes and get back up and try again...and again... and again.

5. Fear of Success

"I FAILED OVER AND OVER AND OVER AGAIN IN MY LIFE.

AND THAT IS WHY I SUCCEED."

- MICHAEL JORDAN

Humans fear achieving success and then losing it. That's entirely possible. Past success is no guarantee of future success. On it's face it sounds kind of silly that anyone would be afraid of success. After all, success is something that we all strive for. Fear of success is closely tied to fear of failure. Human beings in their inexplicable ability to snatch defeat from the jaws of victory have become very adept at playing head games with themselves. "What if I actually achieve the very success that I desire? And what if after achieving the success I somehow manage to lose it?" That is very possible. There are no guarantees that once you achieve success you'll be able to keep it. Getting to the top of the mountain is only half the battle, staying there is the other half.

In many ways humans are creatures of comfort. You find a reality in which you are comfortable and tend to stay there, creating a sense of familiarity, a safe place. Only when you sink below that level does it cause enough discomfort for you to think about acting. I say think about acting because "resting on your laurels" is paired with it's evil twin procrastination- fear of success in action. It looks something like: "I'll get around to ____ because of course I can re-achieve _____." Careful COBRA, nothing in life is a guarantee and you can't always get back to where you once where. A true COBRA strives to exceed their past successes.

Conversely, the thought of leveling up can be terrifying because it's uncharted territory. Humans do not generally like venturing into the unknown. This feeling is often compounded by the negative voice of your inner critic. "Upper management? That's not for me." "I'm not first string material and if I ever made it I'd probably choke during the big game." "Sure, maybe I could get the partner of my dreams to go out with me once, but what if they really got to know me? They'd never stick around." That negative voice reinforces the false thought that you are better off not ever trying because even if you do temporarily succeed, you'll only blow it. You need to step outside of your self and realize that those types of thoughts are garbage and keep you from achieving the success you deserve.

6. Fear of Rejection

"DON'T FEEL BAD IF SOMEONE REJECTS YOU OR IGNORES YOU. PEOPLE USUALLY REJECT AND IGNORE EXPENSIVE THINGS BECAUSE THEY CAN'T AFFORD THEM."

- JULIET VEGA

Rejection doesn't mean you aren't good enough, it means the other person failed to notice what you have to offer. The feeling of rejection arises from your attachment to people, outcomes, feelings and the possibility to lose the connection. When life doesn't reward you with the results you desire or the relationships you "need", fear emerges. You must eliminate qualifying events as either good or bad, instead remain open to the possibility of any number of unforeseen outcomes. You are not going to be everyone's cup of tea. This is a tough pill to swallow, even for me. Auditions have nothing to do with acting, but are the precursor to get an acting job. Many times I have left an audition feeling great, then failed to book the job. In order to face another audition, I had to wrangle myself by applying the Way of the COBRA by remembering, I was not rejected due to my lack of talent, rather I was just not right for the part. When you speculate on the possibility of future calamity you are not living in the present. Knock it off! Stay in the moment, live in gratitude and deal with life as it unfolds.

A COBRA shuns attachment to any specific outcome. This is how you find opportunity even in moments of darkness, chaos and uncertainty, remember the Chinese farmer. When you create a presupposed conclusion based upon inconclusive stimuli you are not living in the present and unable to give 100% effort. Stay out of the results business. Results are beyond your control. A COBRA never forgets that we live in a universe of infinite abundance and endless possibility.

7. Fear of Humiliation

"DO NOT GO WHERE THE PATH MAY LEAD.
GO INSTEAD WHERE THERE IS NO PATH AND
LEAVE A TRAIL."

-RALPH WALDO EMERSON

Few things send a chill up one's spine like the potential for being ridiculed or humiliated in the eyes of our fellow earthlings. This fear can quickly manifest anxiety, insecurity and, worst of all, emotional and even physical paralysis hindering the ability to take chances. Bullying represents one of the most pervasive and destructive forms of humiliation. It has become a crisis in our society. Suicide is the fourth leading cause of death among adolescents. Bullying is one of the largest contributing factors. Bullying leaves scars. It has taken years for mine to fade. A COBRA does not humiliate anyone EVER nor does he tolerate the humiliation of others. The only time that you should fear humiliation is when you've let yourself down, compromised your character and not done your best. Do not give other people the power to subject you to humiliation.

Bullying, ridicule, shame and putting others down are common tactics used by insecure people who haven't developed

58

decent social skills and feel that they are not being seen by others in the way they want to be seen. Acerbic wittiness or mean-spiritedness does not equal smart and funny. Ironically, people who humiliate others often can't handle it when the tables are turned. Meeting rudeness with the same type of behavior drags you down to the other person's level. So tell the person to stop, change the subject or just leave the conversation. Some people will never stop trying to embarrass you in public, no matter what you do. Remember that you can't change people. They have to see the error of their behavior and want to make their own adjustments. As long as you remain poised around these people, the problem is theirs.

There may be a time when someone crosses the line with public humiliation and it becomes bullying. Individual put downs can be interpreted as workplace harassment, and shouldn't be taken lightly. If you feel like you're being harassed at work, know your rights. If you feel that you're a victim of being bullied, stay away from the perpetrator, and if you can't, be prepared to stand up to them, but, make sure you are aware of the consequences.

8. Rational Fear

> "THERE IS A FEAR OUT THERE FOR
> EVERYONE."
>
> - A. D. ALIWAT

You are born with fears programmed into your brain meant to keep you alive. It's the precursor to the hairs standing up on the back of your neck. Fear is primal and gives you the strength to react when faced with an imminent threat, but it can also paralyze you from acting, these are called phobias. Phobias can be rational, like Acrophobia (fear of heights) or irrational like coulrophobia (fear of clowns)... that is unless you knew John Wayne Gacy. Phobias can be treated with a little bit of hard work, just like any fear, and COBRAs aren't afraid of hard work.

The power of fear

There are two great catalysts uniquely responsible for bringing about change within human beings: love and fear. Both emotions form two razor-sharp sides of a double-edged katana. Wars have been waged from both because they hold great power over us; getting us to move mountains, take incredible chances and do things we never believed possible. Fear has the capability to transform you, both positively and negatively.

Everyone experiences fear, and it ain't a pleasant feeling. A little fear can be healthy, while too much renders you paralyzed. You must learn to make an ally of fear and cultivate a warrior mentality; this is absolutely an acquired skill requiring discipline and a significant degree of emotional toughness. Fear can serve as a tool, but you must process fear-provoking stimuli into information. Recognize that fear can drive you, motivate you, and push you beyond the limits created by your mind. Fear isn't the Boogeyman, it lets you know when you're facing impending danger by triggering your "fight or flight" response. We've all heard stories of a petite mother suddenly able to lift a car in order to free her child pinned underneath. Fear of losing her child elicited a physiological response initiating superhuman strength. The clearer you can articulate the origins of your fear, the less your fears will control you.

How the COBRA overcomes fear

When facing a situation that causes anxiety and fear yet does not pose an obvious or immediate physical danger, call a timeout. There's even a chance that you may be having a panic attack. The mind can be a powerful ally or a worthy foe to your physical well-being. Reboot your thought process while centering yourself physically, calm yourself.

• Box breathing

An excellent tool when encountering anything that initiates fear. Breathing brings oxygen to the brain and has an immediate calming effect disrupting the current mindset. Box breathing involves inhaling for a count of four, holding your breath for a count of four. Then exhaling for a count of four and holding your lungs empty for a count of four. Thus creating a "box". Repeat this exercise several times or longer until regain a sense of calm. The results are highly effective and will clear your mind, lower your heart rate and center you.

• Meditation

Begin by sitting in a comfortable position. Keep your back straight and place your tongue on the roof of your mouth. Rest your hands on your thighs with your palms facing upwards.

Align your thumb on top of your index and ring finger in a gentle pinch formation. Your physical position is meant to be complete relaxation free of tension in the body, so adjust as needed for comfort.

Close your eyes or leave them open focusing on a specific point in front of you. It can be a flame, an image or even a blank wall. Clear your mind and detach from any negativity. Concentrate on your breathing. Be aware of the thoughts that intrude, do not chase them. Simply concentrate on your breath as you inhale and exhale.

In the beginning most people can only meditate for a few minutes. With practice you will be able to meditate for longer periods of time reducing the bombardment of intrusive random thoughts. These thoughts or "monkey chatter" represent your bombastic and distracting inner monologue composed of external influences and internal desires, insecurities, anxieties and fears. Meditation will silence the outside world, as well as the monkey chatter, allowing you to achieve calm and presence.

- Control your thoughts

Thoughts are things. What you think about has a direct effect on your physiology and emotions. Be vigilant with your thoughts, unchecked thoughts can generate fear and doubt. All obstacles have their foundation rooted in fear. Fear feeds on doubt and insecurity creating a voice inside which asks "What if I fail?" IGNORE THAT VOICE! It's weak, debilitating and unproductive. Listen to the voice which says "What if I fly?" That's the kind of positive reinforcement you deserve. That's the voice that will propel you to achieve success and personal growth. That is the ONLY voice I want to hear in this dojo.

- Analyze the source of your fear

Take an honest look at the source. Does it come from an external force? First you need to determine the validity of the source. How reliable is the information? There's a big difference in fear inducing information corroborated by multiple reputable sources and some teenage social media influencer's speculation about an asteroid hurtling towards the Earth and ushering in the apocalypse.

- Game out the potential danger

Write down the most likely outcomes then ask yourself how realistic any of them are. You will surely be able to eliminate a few once you look at them with less emotion and more logic.

- Educate yourself

Fear of the unknown is one of the greatest provokers of anxiety. When crossing into unfamiliar territory it is normal to have concerns. Concerns left unchecked can easily degenerate into fear which can lead to panic. Whether you are entering a new field of employment, interacting with an unknown group of people or tackling a daunting new challenge, remember that knowledge is power.

- Remember the three "I's".
1. Investigate - Obtain as much information as possible on the who's, what's, when's and where's.

2. Inform - get informed by searching for information about any challenge that may be foreign to you. Utilize the internet, take a class or a seminar.

3. Inquire - Find an individual who has already walked the path ahead of you. This is the perfect place for a mentor. I will discuss the value of a mentor shortly.

Strike when it is time to strike

"FORTIS FORTUNA ADIUVAT".
(FORTUNE FAVORS THE BOLD.)

-ROMAN PLAYWRIGHT TERENCE

Courage is not the absence of fear but rather the doing of what must be done in the face of fear. Trust your instincts and act. Inaction when action is required creates doubt in yourself and emboldens the aggressive nature in others. A COBRA recognizes that there are moments in life when immediate action is required. There are times when you must strike without hesitation. This may occur in a violent confrontation or in a life or death situation. I'd like to share a story with you about how I overcame one of my phobias.

I *have never been particularly fond of heights. Actually, I have a pretty healthy dislike of elevation, I would classify it as a phobia. I don't suffer from vertigo but all things being equal I prefer maintaining close proximity to terra firma.*

On the morning of my forty second birthday my fear was put to the test. I had reluctantly accepted a job on a reality show that thankfully would not air in the United States. I wasn't particularly happy with my decision to join a documentary about rehab, but frankly I needed the money, so I decided to make the best of it. My other cast mates (which included among others, a couple of over the hill rock stars and a pair of London tabloid queens) and I were constantly presented with surprise challenges. That day was no exception.

I exited the SUV which had taken a group of us high into the Santa Monica mountains of Malibu, California. The raw natural beauty was stunning. Some 800-feet below, the Pacific Ocean slapped against the rocks. Inhaling the crisp mountain air I felt a sense of calm and oneness with my surroundings. That wouldn't last for long. As I turned away from the beautiful landscape my sense of tranquility evaporated almost instantly. My stomach sank and my throat grew tight and dry. Set up above me were an elaborate series of ropes and wires strung amidst various telephone poles. The strange cacophony of wood, hemp and steel formed a daunting obstacle course suspended high overhead. There was also one solitary pole approximately sixty-feet high standing defiantly on its own. It's only companion was a steel trapeze bar suspended six-feet in front, ominously swaying from the November morning breeze. Things were about to get very real, very quickly as I had come face to face with the Confidence Course. The situation certainly inspired a great many emotions, confidence definitely was not one of them. One way or another I was about to confront my fear of heights.

We were all given an explanation of how the safety equipment functioned and then paired together. I was matched up with a young model. So far so good I thought. After a brief moment of mental calculation I surmised that she was young enough or rather I was old enough to be her father. Age seemed to be competing for head-space today along with my growing apprehension of the Confidence Course.

The first assignment seemed relatively benign in the shadow of the lone pole which awaited us at the end of the day. I knew it was coming sooner or later but figured I had better just take things one at a time. Even then I knew it was best to stay in the present.

My partner and I ascended to a small platform high above the ground. Stretched out before us were two wires that began a mere foot apart. Each wire was attached to a pole on one side of us near our dish sized perch where we stood nervously. Fifty feet or so to the other side of us were two more vertical poles where the other ends of the wires were also attached. As the wires approached the distant poles to the other side, the space between them grew until they were over six feet apart. The idea was that we were to stand face to face supporting each other's body weight as we inched our way toward the other side of the course.

Protectively, I focused on my partner's eyes not wanting to look down. She didn't seem very comfortable with this either. I gave her a reassuring smile wondering if she knew how full of it I was. Figuring the best defense in this situation was a good offense. I decided to assume the dominant role as coach/cheerleader. In that moment I learned something interesting about myself. In that period of my life I dealt with my fear by attempting to control the circumstances. I surmised that if could calm my partner's increasing anxiety while motivating her then I wouldn't concentrate on my own fear.

We slowly edged our way towards the other side. Through my peripheral vision I could see the ocean off in the distance below. Directly beneath us were the cast, crew and cameras. It was difficult not to feel self conscious but still we moved further and further towards the other side. The distance between us was rapidly growing and caused us to push harder against each other's hands until we began to assume the shape of an inverted Y. After a few moments I could feel my legs shaking. More intimidating than that was my partner's eroding sense of calm. I tried to reassure her that we were doing just fine. I could see her vulnerability and wanted to take it away and be able to command the situation. I wonder what she thought as she looked into my eyes. We reached an impasse and could no longer move further towards our destination. We both began to teeter and shortly thereafter we plunged to the ground and bounced for a moment or two like a couple of human yo-yos. Fortunately we were belayed by ropes attached to our safety harness. I felt invigorated after the experience. In my mind I had succeeded because I continued until I couldn't continue any further and had given it my best effort. I did not complete the task but I was still able to assign a positive association to the experience because I had met the challenge head on and finished with integrity. I wonder if I could have performed even more effectively had I acknowledged my fear, maybe even admitted it to my partner and let go of the notion that I had to "control" how the experience would unfold. Was I really so caught up in my distorted sense of self and ego that I could not convey my honest emotions? Apparently so.

As I caught my breath, my eyes drifted nervously over to the solitary wooden giant that awaited. In a very short time I was going to have the chance to put my recent observations to practical use. Soon I would face the next challenge. I could feel doubt coursing through my veins. My chest began to pound and I wondered if those around me could sense my abject fear. I wondered if they could tell what I already knew, that this day, the day of my forty second birthday, would either reward me with the fleeting gift of victory or saddle me with the dull, sickening ache of cowardice. So much for living in the present. In retrospect those two options, victory or cowardice only represent two possible emotions that can be attached to the experience. I hadn't considered the benefit of learning from a possible "failure" or attaching a different story to the experience.

I gazed towards the pole and in that moment had two very distinct and very clear realizations. First, I was genuinely scared. Less from the obstacle before me and more from the knowledge of how I would forever view myself if I couldn't fully commit and give what I knew was my honest and best effort. Secondly, compared to the previous challenge which I had not completed, the one that awaited appeared exponentially more difficult and dangerous. The moment of truth had arrived. The instructor surveyed the group sizing up each of us. "Who's first?" I blurted out, "I am". How the hell did that just happen? Like a bell can't be unrung, neither could those words once they escaped.

I screwed on my best game face and after a quick check of my safety rig I started my ascent. The cast and crew assembled at the base of the lone telephone pole. I looked upward, the sixty-foot tall pole was lined with iron pegs for climbing to the top. The wind had started picking up and I had serious misgivings about my ability to scale the pole let alone stand atop its tiny surface area and then throw myself towards the trapeze bar which hovered six feet away and then catch it. The cast cheered me on as I climbed step after step. About three quarters of the way up, I realized the wind was becoming a real factor.

Finally after what seemed like an interminably long amount of time my hand reached the top. Now I needed to hoist myself up and onto the top. I took a moment to catch my breath and digest the realization that the surface area was about the size of a salad plate. Quickly I tried to calculate the best way to move from my current situation, not unlike that of a Koala bear hugging a eucalyptus tree, to a standing position. I could feel fatigue spreading through my upper body. I sensed the growing impatience of the cast and crew below me. More disturbing were my thoughts that I simply couldn't figure out how to lift my body up and onto this tiny surface area. After several minutes I made my move. I managed to plant one of my feet but it took a tremendous amount of energy to step up with my other leg. I pushed with everything I had and after struggling for a few tense seconds, I stood up. Within an instant I had gone from desperation, clinging to the side of the pole to liberation as I stood on top and looked out across the mountains and the ocean below. I felt a brief moment of triumph and accomplishment.

Within a very short time however I was brought back to reality as I watched the trapeze swing before me. It was not blowing back and forth violently. Just enough to create an additional and significant obstacle to the challenge. The view of the ocean in front of me and about 800 feet below only enhanced the sensation of being high above the ground. I drew a deep breath and remember very clearly what I was thinking in that moment. "Let go." Let go of all my fear and hand it over to the universe which will not let me fall but will support me. I knew that making this leap towards the trapeze was really a leap of faith for me. It was a metaphor for leaving behind old fears and attachments. Rather than concentrate on what could happen or how I would feel if I failed, I focused on how incredible it would feel to just go for it with total abandon. I suddenly felt a sense of freedom I had never known before. I launched myself towards the cross bar of the trapeze with everything I had. I immediately felt the cold steel in my hands. It took a split second to realize that I was not going to lose my grip. I cannot describe with words alone the feeling of oneness and harmony that I felt in the instant when I knew I had succeeded. It was sublime. I could not have asked for a better gift from the universe on my forty-second birthday.

YOUR INNER CRITIC

HEED THE WORDS OF YOUR INNER
GENIUS. IGNORE THE WORDS OF
YOUR INNER CRITIC.

What is the inner critic?

The inner critic is a hungry little beast that lives in our psyche, collecting ridicule, harsh criticism and our perceived "failures" then projects them back on us with cutting ferocity. Here's the kicker,the inner critic actually means well but has horrendous communication skills. It tries to let you know when something's really important or when it's crunch time. Unfortunately it does this in a very destructive way using demeaning words and defeatist phrases.

Technically speaking the inner critic is a false reality you constructed from your personal history. It draws from the library of your past experiences, specifically when you were exposed to damaging and intentionally or unintentionally abusive behavior. Generally, this occurs at a very young and impressionable age. Unfortunately the culprits tend to be those people closest to us.

Good news, bad news, again. First the bad news: We all have an inner critic and it always seems to rear its ugly head at precisely the moment we need to feel confident, secure and empowered. The inner critic manifests as that negative, repetitive and taunting voice inside saying "You aren't good enough, don't deserve love, happiness and success and will never have it" or some variation of that. Heading into an important meeting? Looking in the mirror while getting ready for a first date? That's usually when the negative tape starts playing.

Now the good news. There is a solution for dealing with the inner critic. I'm gonna show you how to identify that voice, call it out and kick it's ass. First, by revealing the inner critic's source of power: your perceived past "failures". Then I'm going to show you how to rewire your perception of those events, make them work for you and reclaim your power.

How does the inner critic grow?

Our psyche is not unlike our muscles. When we go to the gym and lift weights we are actually tearing down the muscle. By providing the muscle with good nutrition, specifically protein, ample recuperation through sleep and consistent repetition, we build the muscle through scarring and it becomes bigger and stronger. Same with our inner critic. The inner critic thrives when we attach negative thoughts and feelings to all of the "negative" experiences and "failures" amassed over a lifetime in which we have failed to grow and learn. Neglecting to learn and evolve from these past experiences is the only true failure.

Negative associations link to "failure", or what we believe constitutes "failure", because it originates from the destructive criticism and negative comments perpetrated against us. This results in toxic shame. Every time you attempt something resulting in a negative outcome and then attach a negative meaning to the experience producing toxic shame, you create a doorway for the inner critic to emerge. When you attempt something, or anything, and "fail" then attach a negative story to the result, you have effectively made your inner critic stronger. Next time you try something new and out of your comfort zone, the inner critic's voice becomes louder and more powerful. So COBRA, you must wrangle your inner critic because there is no room in this dojo for a harsh critic. You wouldn't let anyone else talk to you like that, so don't do it to yourself.

That doesn't mean that COBRAs never feel the sting of what I call "healthy" shame. (Healthy shame is triggered when you don't try your best or at all.) Shame can be a powerful catalyst as long as it's not toxic shame. Healthy loss and shame teach you what you don't want to feel again. They motivate and inspire you. Healthy shame is like touching a hot stove, it reminds you of the pain you felt from a result different from the one that you desire. By not allowing perceived "failure" to degenerate into toxic shame, you rob the inner critic of its food and weaken its voice.

COBRAs as a rule, don't allow their inner critic to produce toxic shame that plunges them into victimhood. Allow me to clarify something for you right here and now: **You do not have to be a victim.** This is not the old days when basic survival was extremely difficult and left you very little opportunity to protect yourself nor remove yourself from negativity. Next time you find yourself playing the victim, remember you have the incredible good fortune to be born at a time when there are more technological and medical advancements, access to convenience, transportation and food than ever before. Humans are living longer and healthier lives with an ever increasing access to knowledge, information and opportunity. In short, you don't have it so bad. Repeat after me: A COBRA IS NOT A VICTIM.

Find value in "failure"

It's imperative that you find value in "failure" which isn't really failure at all. Society has become so afraid of casting the shadow of shame upon anyone that it has adopted a philosophy of "everyone's a winner" just for showing up. Well, guess what? Life in the real world doesn't work that way and life in this dojo doesn't work that way. A COBRA doesn't need a trophy for sixth place because it causes you to become entitled and mediocre.

Don't get me wrong. Winning is definitely better than losing. Succeeding is absolutely more gratifying than failing. I don't care if you're Tom Brady or Michael Jordan, everyone experiences both. COBRAs turn "loss" and "failure" into motivation. How you deal with failure is a major determinant in your character. Everyone gets knocked down. How you react and your ability to get back up makes all the difference. Don't listen when the inner critic starts telling you that maybe you're not meant for success. Everyone is meant for success, it's up to you to claim it. Remember the fifth pillar of *Way of the COBRA*: we live in a world of ABUNDANCE.

Attach positive meaning to "failure"

Begin by ceasing to use the word "failure". From now on we will call it an "alternative and temporary outcome because we are unable to see what the future holds". Remember the words of the wise, Chinese farmer, "We shall see." Frequently unwanted outcomes prepare us for future success or free us up for something even better. That doesn't mean you should accept "failure" and give up, it just means you need to re-adjust your thinking to accept the outcome or approach the goal in a different way.

I am divorced and now happily remarried. At the time when my first marriage collapsed, I descended into the belly of the beast, facing uncertainty and crushing heartache. It was one of the lowest points in my life. Admittedly, it's hard not to view divorce as the F-word. Mine generated a great deal of toxic shame and fed my hungry inner critic like an all-you-can-eat buffet. If only I had heard the words of the Chinese farmer. If only I could have looked past my immediate circumstance and understood that what appeared and felt like crisis actually represented opportunity. In fact, the conclusion of my first marriage ultimately allowed me to meet my soulmate, fall in love, get married with a beautiful wedding in Italy and embark upon the greatest adventure of my life.

That happened as a direct result of my toxic shame evolving into a healthier form of shame. When faced with any type of outcome it's imperative that you work to create a positive association rather than a negative one based on toxic shame. Sometimes you can achieve this quickly (I'm not saying that it happens instantly) and other times it develops over time like in the case of my divorce. It pushed me to work on myself. I had to fight my way through an emotional wasteland and it wasn't a vertical path to the promised land. I took a long, hard and honest look at the outcome from my defunct marriage. I considered the mistakes that I had made and the way I allowed myself to be treated. I decided if I ever married again I would be the best husband possible. I never wanted to hear the cutting words from my inner critic telling me that no one would ever love me and that I didn't deserve to be happy. The failure of my first marriage had effectively become a teacher and a cautionary tale rather than a source of shame and pain.

Another source of outcome is your career. You may love your job like me, but they call it work for a reason. The majority of an actor's professional career is the quest to find work rather than actually working. This involves auditioning and, very frequently, rejection. More often than not, I don't get the part. Linking a positive association to an audition that doesn't turn into a job is critical for me. If I allowed myself to view every audition in which I didn't get the role as a failure I would feel unsuccessful for a large part of my existence.

Assuming that I have done my best with the material, and I'll be honest, even I have an off-day, I always look for the positive aspect of the experience. Maybe I had the opportunity to audition for a group of people who were previously unaware of my work. These are now people who saw me give a great reading and will remember me for future roles. Maybe I wasn't meant to get the role because I am supposed to be available for something bigger and more important. Whatever the case I attach a positive association to the experience. If I tanked the audition I do a self-diagnostic.

Was I adequately prepared? Did I allow external distractions to affect my performance? Was my script analysis off base? Asking myself these questions allows me to create a positive association with the experience. Conversely if I gave a great audition I also attach a positive story. I just wasn't right for the role and it had nothing to do with my talent. If I didn't do this my inner critic would have so much ammo, I wouldn't be able to step foot into another audition.

Give your inner critic an identity

Assign your inner critic a name and find something absurd to represent it. It can be an action figure, a stuffed animal or a picture. Keep it handy, look at it or just mentally envision it. I know it sounds silly, that's the idea! I envision my inner critic is a petulant little boy named Timmy. When Timmy doesn't get what he wants, which is undermining my sense of confidence and self-worth, he begins taunting me with his arsenal of negative insults.

I have an agreement with Timmy. When he decides to make an appearance I tolerate him for few seconds. He tries to tell me all the reasons why I always screw up *this* or never succeed at *that*. The more I resist, the more of a brat he becomes throwing a tantrum. I wind up laughing at how silly he is, then tell him to shut up and send him on his way. This invariably brings a smile to my face and in turn, changes my entire state both mentally and physically. I feel reinvigorated and ready to attack the next challenge. I do this by utilizing the... the three "R's"

- REALIZE - the inner critic's voice does not reflect reality.

Emotionally charged words like "always" and "never" rarely apply in life when it comes to human behavior. Verbal absolutes are often used to create inaccurate one-sided narratives. When you begin hearing these words in your head mentally stop and recognize it's your inner critic not reality. It's time to shut it down and reboot. You do this by changing your state of mind which will in turn change your physical sense of well being.

- REBOOT - Shut down the negativity and change your state.

Simply change your environment in any way practical. Even going to the restroom to splash water on your face can be enough.

Meditation can help quiet your mind if Timmy's psyching you out before something important. I like to listen to music that either fires me up or calms me down. If little Timmy has you all riled up or you are angry, exercise! It's the best and fastest way to silence that little beast. So take a contemplative walk or run him out like they do to horses in heat.

- REFOCUS - Time to get back in the game.

Ask yourself what advice you would give your younger self in the same circumstances. You would be supportive and encouraging, not critical and demeaning. This is the time to enlist the help of a friend or mentor if you can't come up with a solution on your own. Take that positive advice and refocus your energy, commitment, and resolve.

Eliminate internal negativity

Are you tired of being dismissed, marginalized, put down and criticized? Then stop doing it to yourself.

```
STICKS AND STONES BREAK MY BONES
BUT WORDS WILL NEVER HURT ME.
```

This children's rhyme leaves a lot to be desired when it comes to the real world. Be vigilant with the words you use to others but also how you talk to yourself. Life is hard enough. The world has no shortage of haters, doubters, detractors and naysayers who will put you down and minimize your light and voice without *you* giving them a hand by allowing your inner critic to use you as a psychic punching bag. Like when you mutter to yourself "what an idiot" after you make a mistake. We have all done it at one time or another.

Conversely have you ever cheered for yourself with an "attaboy" or "I'm killing it"? Good job COBRA!! Think about the state you were in when you were saying these very different phrases to yourself. It's very simple. You can either act as a heckler or a cheerleader. Given the choice, I'll go with the cheerleader. It's easier said than done, but Rome wasn't built in a day, but it's still around. So take the time to learn this new habit, you're worth it.

Eliminate external negativity

How many times have you wanted to attempt something

new or possibly again after a negative outcome only to hear those people closest to you say "come on, you couldn't possibly do that" or " you're too old or too young" or "blah, blah, blah"? Often the very people whom we love and who love us have no problem verbalizing their negativity which ignites our inner critic. Nothing gets the critic fired up like the doubting words from a mother, a father or a mate. They almost always come in the form of gentle and loving counsel. Because we care for the people who are voicing the negativity we tend to take it straight to heart. Oh, man does the inner critic love this!

There is a profound yet often subtle difference between constructive criticism and the projection of the limiting beliefs of others. You must be the judge and determine motivation and accuracy behind the unsolicited advice, after all, most loved ones want to see you succeed. But if you determine that everyone around you is trumpeting the same thing... chances are you may need to take another look. But, if it's just a few haters, like your mother-in-law who wanted her golden child to marry someone else, then you must immediately distance yourself from this type of negativity. It is an unfortunate fact of life that very often other people feel threatened when we attempt to break out of our comfort zone and break through a psychological ceiling. Often our attempts to do this serve as an unflattering reflection of their inability to do the same. A COBRA doesn't allow the fears of others, even loved ones, to dictate a ceiling for our potential.

MAKE PEACE WITH YOUR INNER CHILD

"SO, LIKE A FORGOTTEN FIRE, A CHILDHOOD CAN ALWAYS FLARE UP AGAIN WITHIN US."

~GASTON BACHELARD

Our inner child serves as the source from which we draw creativity and inspiration. Both fuel self-worth and vitality; integral components of happiness. The actual term "inner child" was coined around 1963 by author Dr. W. Hugh Missildine in his book "*Your Inner Child of the Past*", where he wrote, "Children learn what they live." If that's true then many of us have learned at the hands of some very cruel and shaming teachers.

The term "Inner Child" has evolved into a representation or, better yet, a personification of our actual source of psychic pain and sadness. Your inner child serves as a receptacle for toxic shame accrued during your childhood at your most vulnerable. COBRAs don't allow previous events to dictate their future. It's time to reconcile the past, kick victimhood to the curb and make peace with this little kid who holds so much power over you. This doesn't mean forget or bury your past pain, it means forgive and move on.

People may have two negative relationships with their inner child. First, they recall the trauma inflicted upon them as children. I call this fear. Secondly, and equally unfortunate, their inner child becomes an object of self hatred, viewed as weak and impotent in the face of mistreatment. Usually accompanied with scalding judgments of our inner critic. Fear and our inner critic share a very intimate relationship with our inner child and are fueled by the same experiences that create our inner child. The negative experiences of our youth can create horrible wounds, whereas the positive ones tend to be ignored or cherry-picked for the negatives. Don't ask my why, but if I had to guess, it's the same reason that nasty stories sell newspapers... ok Millennials, it's the same reason we sit in traffic: so people can stare at an accident as they pass.

Some wounds have healed with time, life experience and love. Others unfortunately remain open and have festered causing pain and block your inner badass. The moment has come to heal your pain, and learn to love rather than loathe your inner child. I'd like to tell you a story **SPOILER ALERT** it comes from my childhood.

Third-Grader Sean knew the danger in stopping but his chest was pounding and he was exhausted. He opted to hide behind a very short wall made of flagstone instead of the "Green Giant", the massive green dumpster only a few yards further away. Although not tall for his age, he struggled to crouch down and draw his knees into his still pounding chest. Compressing his chubby eight-year-old frame was painful but he had to be certain that they wouldn't see him just long enough to catch his breath. He removed his thick glasses to blot the perspiration dripping from his brow burning his eyes.

He fumbled with his eyeglasses for a moment deciding whether or not to put them back on his face. He hated his glasses and the taunts that they inspired. They were a constant source of anxiety, not because he couldn't see very well without them, he couldn't; (at least not well enough to fight), but because leaving them on represented a legitimate danger if he was punched in the face. He stared at the glasses for a beat then drew a deep breath and put them squarely on his face.

Unfortunately, he had made a mistake, his fear had caused him to miscalculate. The wall, while long, was barely three feet high and didn't offer nearly as much cover as the "Green Giant". He knew it was a temporary fix, because he was within striking distance of his home and had a decent chance of making it if he could just catch his breath. But had the older boys chasing him cut behind the school so that they could wait for him in the parking lot?

That parking lot was a sea of black asphalt about fifty yards long but that day it seemed like a million. Fifty yards; 150 feet. That was the distance separating him from the safety of his front yard. Young Sean knew that if he was going to make it he would have to risk sticking his head above the wall. At least long enough to check and see if those bullies had tricked him by allowing him to think that he was safe in his hiding spot so they could catch up. There simply was no other way. Slowly he raised his head above the wall. Immediately he felt a lump in his throat. They were there.

There must have been at least eight or ten of them, bullies standing around just waiting to pounce on him, a younger kid. Some of them were even wearing leather jackets, and one of them was smoking. They would have been "cool" if they weren't trying to pick an unfair fight. For a split second young Sean actually forgot how scared he was and wished that just once he could wear one of those cool brown leather jackets.

Young Sean had made it before. In fact he had made it many times but not always. On those days when he hadn't been so lucky he never knew what to expect. Most times it was just a chorus of humiliating insults. The kind that an eight-year-old boy struggles to understand coming from older boys and usually reference his mother. Even though he didn't always understand, he knew they were meant to insult him, badly. Bad enough to make the back of his neck hot and red. Bad enough to make him wish that he was taller, older or stronger so that he could fight... not in vengeance but because sometimes it was worse than just the nasty words and name calling. This was shaping up to be one of those times.

He knew he would have about three, maybe four, seconds (if he was lucky) before they would see him. If he ran with every ounce of fear that coursed through his body, he had a decent chance of making it to his front door. They had never dared to actually step off the sidewalk in front of his house. They wouldn't come onto the front lawn, would they? Worse than the fear that the boys would catch him, was the fear that they would chase him all the way home. The fear that his father would decide that today he wanted to eat lunch at home instead of downtown. That his dad would finally learn how his son spent his lunch time.

I honestly don't remember if I made it home that day or not. I do know that as I wrote these words I was overcome with a profound sadness for that little guy, which is a switch for me. For years I carried with me a distorted image of that scared and victimized little boy--my loser inner child. I hated him. I hated his weakness and inability to stand up for himself. I judged him for being a coward. I spent years in the gym and the karate dojo to harden my body and my spirit, which allowed me to protect him.

Protecting him seemed like the right thing to do, after all, he is the building block for my self-esteem.

But it took decades of introspection and therapy to soften my emotions toward my vulnerable inner child. Not very COBRA-like of me... I know, but as Bryan Adams so eloquently sang... the first cut is the deepest. Ok Gen X-ers, Rod Stewart covered it. And Gen Y-ers Sheryl Crow covered it too. You happy Millennials? I know you fact checked it. But it's true, our inner child learns everything it needs to know by the time you're ten years old and you spend the rest of your time correcting it. For me, it wasn't until my wife, a very wise COBRA, clued me into a whole new way of living by looking at the world with the words:

"I LOVE YOU BECAUSE OF YOU,
NOT IN SPITE OF YOU."

These magic words will change your life too. If you have someone in your life that you can say them to, they will elevate your relationship to a new dimension of trust and understanding. If that someone says them to you, they are probably a COBRA. But keep reading, because saying and hearing those words is just the beginning. You need to accept them and live them-- for your inner child-- so you can draw strength and inspiration from the little guy. To do so, you must heal your inner child. Only then can you hope to become a COBRA. Let the healing begin.

The first step involves identification and has two parts:

1. Make a visual identification of your inner child so that it becomes concrete and tangible.

We all hold a very specific and clear image of our inner child... including me. If you do not, create one so that you can heal. There are many ways of doing this, I recommend old photographs. Select one that matches your mental image. Be creative so you represent all of the negative aspects of your inner child. Maybe it's an object that represents rather than resembles the image in your head. It could be a baseball glove or an item of clothing. Whatever allows you to get in touch and feel connected to that hater in your head.

2. Identify your current relationship to your inner child.

This part is trickier because it demands you take a good

77

long look in the mirror while having an honest conversation about which category your inner child falls into : victim or pariah.

Victim Category

Your inner child is so deeply wounded that it requires constant nurturing. You even employ your victimhood as a way to receive "benefits" like sympathy or pity. At least initially, you find that people are willing to listen to your sad stories which serves as your method to connect. Most of your social interactions revolve around people coddling your inner victim, but you find that when you check your inbox there are no invites to game night. Be honest COBRA, this is not a judgment. Stay focused, your inner badass is trapped behind this internal obstacle. You are done playing the victim.

You will notice that I wrote "playing" the victim because it can be just that, a role chosen. Obviously there is a spectrum of severity and frequency. Everyone gets tired of "flying the COBRA flag" from time to time and falls into this pattern... even me... well, especially me (I am an actor and I do make my living being dramatic, so it comes with the territory). COBRAs soon realize the error of their ways and set out to correct their course, mostly by re-reading this book.

Now this is not to say, in **any** way, that people who have undergone trauma were not victims when the trauma occurred. Not only were they victims, but they are heroes for surviving. If you fall into that category, you are a COBRA for reading this book. Thank you for surviving so that you could join my dojo. Journal your progress and share your success with me through my website. If the steps in this book get too tough, pause and get professional help. Your seat will be saved until you are ready to continue. This book is meant to inspire you to keep going until your inner badass is unleashed from the trauma. There is no shame in asking for professional help to heal the damage caused by trauma. People who seek the help of support groups in an attempt to understand their woundedness do not constitute victims in this dojo.

Colin Tipping, founder and director of the Institute for Radical Forgiveness and Coaching Therapy, developed a therapy called "Radical Forgiveness". It releases the individual from the need to cling to his or her "woundedness" in order to eliminate self perpetuated victimhood. "Clinging on" to your woundedness can mark an unhealthy and frequently destructive attachment. If you are not a trauma survivor, or you are years into therapy, but cling to pain in an unhealthy way and as a way to garner sympathy, you are actively choosing to play a role.

COBRAS ARE NOT VICTIMS.

We all have psychic scars, that's part of what makes us human. The proactive decision to heal and reconcile differentiates you from wallowing in victimhood. That healing may take quite some time but honest self examination and the sincere desire to heal yourself makes you a winner in my dojo.

Pariah Category

Banishing your inner child as a way of defending against the pain that it's presence generates puts you, or rather your inner child, in the pariah category. However completely eliminating attachment to your pain may actually prove short sighted, like throwing out the baby with the bath water. You need pain to remind you not to repeat your mistakes and to force you to grow. As an actor I frequently draw on psychic pain to inform emotional choices. While it's definitely not a comfortable feeling it is effective. You need to learn how to make them work for you. Your woundedness or inner child represents one of the most integral parts that collectively make up the sum of your being and define who you are as an individual. Your inner child is fundamentally necessary to your existence. That's why you must seek to understand it rather than dismiss it.

I must now make a confession to you; I have a dark side. You do too. Think of that dark side as one of many facets of your inner child. While not always pretty, convenient or desirable it is nonetheless a part of each and every one of us and indispensable. You cannot simply cast it aside. You must endeavor to understand it and embrace it. Much of your strength and creativity flows from the sources of your pain, your "woundedness". The secret lies, not in ignoring your inner child nor in clinging to it or more accurately clinging to the stories you have attached to it but rather, in freeing your inner child from the burden of carrying a lifetime of pain and welcoming it to a place of peace and understanding.

How do you, not only achieve peace with your inner child but, utilize it? How do you integrate it among the rest of your personality so that it can serve you in a positive way, rather than existing as a source of destructive pain that requires you to constantly nurture it almost ensuring a cycle self victimization? I wish the answer was complex and I wish that it was original and that I could take credit for it but it's not. The simple answer, like so many others, is love. You must love a part of yourself which has seemed unlovable. How do you do this?

1. Your inner child is not who you **are**, but rather, a **part** of who you are.

Even if you continue to struggle with pain and trauma that you associate with your inner child, you have evolved beyond the inner child itself. You've grown through life experience, relationships etc. To reduce yourself, as an adult, to a distorted image of your inner child would not only be an unfair mistake, it would be inaccurate. That simply is not who you are today.

Remember that tangible representation of your inner child that I asked you to create? I would like you to pick it up and stare at it for a moment. Now say out loud "You are not the sum total of who I am. You are a part of me that I love and need. However, you are not the sum total of who I am today." You purchased this book, obviously you are either one of my family members or you are genuinely interested in improving. So, put your ego aside and look at the representation of your inner child and repeat aloud the words. Do this several times, several times a day until you believe it. "Fake it 'til you make it". If this means that you carry your inner child representation with you for a while then so be it. This is your precious life, there is no dress rehearsal so who gives a damn what anyone else thinks. This is about you. Be selfish. You are worth it.

2. Forgiveness presents you with an emotional two-way street.

You must not only ask for it from your inner child but open yourself up to accepting it. For what exactly must you ask forgiveness? The simple answer rests in the anger that you carry around like a heavy set of chains. Some of us wear these chains with defiance, proclaiming a desire to end the pain that hobbles us. Still others display them like a reluctant badge of courage and source of identification. Often this is done so that we may recognize others whose inner children share similar qualities. This allows us to bond through mutual woundedness.

But from where does this anger originate? It is important to understand that your anger is directed at the image of your inner child as well as your adult self. Initially your anger towards your inner child, yourself, centers around the inner child's impotence and lack of facility to resolve the traumatic problems that confronted it. Whether it was the inability to stand up to bullies or the failure to protect a mother from the abuse of a raging, alcoholic father. You are angry because you were unable to resolve a traumatic problem which has caused you terrible pain. This anger is directed at the embodiment of your pain and woundedness, a defenseless "child".

That anger then generates a separate rage towards not only your inner child but your adult self. You are furious that your inner child has made you feel guilty and impotent by placing you in an untenable position. The inner child, unable to fend for itself, required your protection which you were unable to provide. Surely now as a capable adult you would have been able to protect and help your inner child if only you were there. Logic tells us that simply wasn't possible but does little to relieve your sense of shame. The majority of us do not like the emotions associated with an inability to protect those we love including ourselves. I say the majority because unfortunately there exists a part of the population that derives some misplaced sense of pleasure or connection from the negative feelings it produces. These feelings allow some to beat up upon themselves and play the victim which functions as a quest for sympathy. That serves as a form of connection for them.

You must also ask forgiveness for having thrust upon your inner child the burden of carrying your pain for all these years. In reality, you would never ask an actual child to shoulder such an enormous responsibility yet you think nothing of subjecting yourself to the monumental task.

How do you actually perform the act of asking for forgiveness? Simply say or write the words. Take the photo or whatever object you chose to represent your inner child and place it before you. Simply speak from the heart and say something like "I did the best I could. I am sorry if I wasn't able to give you everything you needed. Please forgive me." If you choose to write a letter to your inner child I suggest that you put it away for a few hours after completing it. Later, take it to a quiet place, maybe the beach. Read it aloud then burn it and be done with it.

3. Accept forgiveness.

Now possibly the most difficult part of this process. You must feel deep within yourself that you have freed your inner child from the prison of pain that surrounded it. You must acknowledge that while there were times that you used your inner child as a scapegoat and an excuse, those days are over. From now on you will see your inner child for who it really is. A part of you from long ago that no longer defines who you are. You have no need to over nurture it nor do you need to shun it. Accept your inner child for who it is. You have freed one and other. Welcome it to join you in a healthy way that will provide you with strength and inspiration to release your inner badass.

SELF-DISCIPLINE

"IF YOU WISH TO BE OUT FRONT,
THEN ACT AS IF YOU WERE
BEHIND."
- LAO TZU

Self-discipline, or rather a lack thereof, presents a significant obstacle for most people, it requires imposing willpower over desire. Humans struggle with this because willpower is a learned attribute opposite our default: the desire for pleasure, comfort and gratification. Our current culture, where so much is available to us with such ease, heightens the desire-train with instant gratification and sound-bite communication. Harnessing the skill of self-discipline makes all the difference in EVERYTHING, it's the absolute foundation on which success is built and a quality every COBRA demonstrates. No one who achieves any notable and lasting success has done so without self-discipline.

You need to understand the difference between discipline and self-discipline. While they share certain qualities there is one major differentiation. Discipline is dispensed from an external force whereas self-discipline is summoned from within us. It already exists within you but may need to be revived or even restored. It should have been instilled by your parents and refined with experience. I can and will teach you strategies for re-engaging it within yourself and employing it in your life. Make no mistake, discipline can produce very positive results. However when the external force of discipline is no longer present, there is no guarantee that disciplined-induced behavior will continue.

Discipline starts in the crib, when tiny white belts cry to have their needs met. The maternal instinct kicks in and figures out what the baby needs forming trust and rudimentary communication. When it goes well and the baby only cries to get his needs met, self-discipline is born. However, when it doesn't go well... self-discipline gets shuffled to the back of the deck behind discipline. As teens, self-discipline gets another bite at the apple, but if it doesn't go well... the military usually picks up the slack or in severe cases, the criminal justice system.

Discipline in the military creates highly trained, organized and command responsive soldiers for as long as they are enlisted. Yet, the twenty-year old marine in peak physical condition often becomes the overweight middle-aged couch potato with the removal of discipline. The prison system exerts order over the potential for dangerous chaos. Yet, once back in the free world and no longer subjected to the harsh discipline of incarceration, many dangerous ex-cons re-offend.

This is not to say that there aren't ex-military, as well as, ex-cons who retain the positive attributes of their training. Those who possess, or have learned, self-discipline in tandem with the disciplined environment no longer require an external force to compel them to adhere to a code of behavior because they hold themselves accountable. Simply put, discipline is like working out with a personal trainer. You can absolutely achieve great results as the trainer pushes you, guides you and supports you. But self-discipline requires you absorb the information given, then you train on your own because you have your own motivation to do so rather than a fear of getting into trouble if you don't.

Why is self-discipline important?

It compels you to finish what you start, complete tasks and reach goals. The more goals you reach the more success you achieve. Self-discipline enforces consistency. Consistency breeds improvement. With few exceptions, the more you practice something over time the better you become.

> *About two years ago I began studying Mandarin. In the beginning the strange written characters and foreign sounds were utterly incomprehensible. Now after over a year of private lessons I can say I've made some significant progress. Don't get me wrong it's all still pretty incomprehensible but incrementally less every week. Consistency is a by-product of self-discipline and pays off over time.*
>
> *Now you may be thinking "But wait, Sensei. Didn't you say that using a trainer, or in your case a teacher, constitutes discipline and not self-discipline?" And I would say "Give me a break, it's Mandarin, CHINESE!"*

A lack of self-discipline makes it impossible to have true

peace and harmony in your life. Without peace and harmony you will not realize your goals, allow your inner badass to emerge and achieve lasting success. In short, you will not become a COBRA. Allow me to break it down.

Suffering comes from the pursuit of fleeting sensory pleasure and attachment to material possessions and results. I call this pursuit "filling the whole". No, I didn't misspell a word. This is an attempt to make yourself feel whole by filling an emptiness with temporary "pleasures". Whether it's food, alcohol, drugs, retail therapy or empty sex, none of it will bring lasting peace and harmony. It feels good and satisfying in the moment but just as quickly it evaporates like a snowflake in the warm palm of your hand. It's a sucker's game, the emptiness returns and the cycle of pursuit begins again, creating an unquenchable emotional thirst and suffering. Self-discipline is the chariot which carries you across the battlefield of temptation. The release of attachment is the strategy which allows you to conquer the army of suffering.

"THERE IS ONLY ONE WAY TO SUCCEED IN ANYTHING... AND THAT IS TO GIVE IT EVERYTHING."

- VINCE LOMBARDI

Meditation is an excellent way to not only reduce fear but diffuse the antagonizing pull of self serving cravings. Does it always work? No. Is my life better because I meditate on these words? Absolutely. I'm a big fan of the "fake it till you make it" school of thought. Be aspirational. What begins as going through the motions through consistent repetition will take root and bare fruit. These are the words upon which I meditate to still my mind and quiet the voice inside that always demands more. Read these words several times. Contemplate them, come back to them. They have had a profound effect on me and are, in fact, echo indirectly to the story of the Chinese farmer. Remember, everything is interconnected.

The passage below is from the Bhagavad Gita which is an epic second century poem from Vyasa originally in Sanskrit. If you have the time and the self-discipline, add this to your reading list, it's an oldie, but a goodie. Faced with going to battle against his kinsman, young Prince Arjuna wrestles with doubt and fear. Lord Krishna explains that all battles begin in the mind and must be won there before they may be won on the battlefield.

Arjuna:

Tell me of the man who lives in wisdom.
Ever aware of the Self, O Krishna;
How does he talk, how sit, how move about?

Sri Krishna:

"He lives in wisdom Who sees himself in all and all in him,
Whose love for the Lord of Love has consumed.
Every selfish desire and sense-craving
Tormenting the heart. Not agitated
By grief nor hankering after pleasure,
He lives free from lust and fear and anger
Fettered no more by selfish attachments,
He is not elated by good fortune
Nor depressed by bad. Such is the seer."
When you keep thinking about sense-objects,
Attachment comes. Attachment breeds desire,
The lust of possession which, when thwarted,
Burns to anger. Anger clouds the judgment
And robs you of the power to learn from past mistakes
Lost is the discriminative faculty,
And your life is utter waste.
But when you move amidst the world of sense
From both attachment and aversion freed,
There comes the peace in which all sorrows end,
And you live in the wisdom of the Self."

The wisdom of these words is absolutely undeniable. The steadfast adherence to them presents a constant and never-ending challenge. At least it does for me. Remember that happiness is a journey rather than a destination. All we can do is keep on truckin'. Now, before you ask me in which cave on what mountain in Kathmandu I reside, let me tell you that I too struggle with temptations and desires that surround all of us. I am beyond fortunate to love and be loved by my incredible wife, Michele, and not succumb to the temptation of others. The fact that I have a healthy dose of fear of her probably helps. Her "karate" is definitely not a joke.

I certainly struggle with my own cage of monkeys. Generally they come in the form of the siren song of the refrigerator at midnight. The point, is that we all have our struggles. Different battles, same war. It's a constant battle to maintain self-discipline and focus. As you level up, problems do not go away. You get new ones that will test you all the time. The ability to maintain self-discipline, balance, character and all of the other attributes found in a COBRA are refined in the struggle.

Embrace the struggle, it will show you who you are. It will develop your character as you become stronger and more adept at handling new challenges, obstacles and temptations. They don't stop coming, but the path to peace and happiness involves extinguishing unhealthy and selfish desires to follow the middle path like the Samurai when drinking Sake:

ONE SIP IS IMPETUOUS. THREE IS TREPIDATIOUS. TWO SIPS ARE THAT OF A SELF-DISCIPLINED SAMURAI.

Enemies of self discipline

COBRAs recognize and implement solid strategies to cultivate self-discipline. These five Horsemen of the Apocalypse seek to undermine self-discipline at every turn. They are...

1. Scheduling - Time management requires self-discipline. The inability to properly marshal time dramatically reduces productivity which leads to unrealized goals and diminished success.

2. Laziness - The ability to act upon a necessary task but not the will to do so. If you are indeed lazy there is little help or hope for you. Fortunately, given the fact that you are reading this book, I am inclined to believe you are not lazy.

3. Procrastination - putting off what needs to be done assuming there will always be more time. Here's a newsflash: we don't know how much time we have left.

4. Delay - Failing to act because circumstances are not ideal. Circumstances are NEVER ideal.

5. Talent - Natural ability or skill. That's right. Talent is a gift from the divine however it can be a damaging curse.

If you are blessed to have been gifted talent in any area but believe this excuses you from hard work then you are sorely mistaken. Self-discipline and hard work will defeat talent when talent is lazy. Self-discipline and hard work will triumph over talent when talent foolishly believes that is sufficient. Trust me, it is not. I am fortunate to have talent in certain areas. When I have been arrogant and believed that I was innately more capable because of that I lost. Conversely, I have competed with individuals who possessed more raw talent than I however I worked harder and I won. When talent combines with self-discipline the combination is usually unstoppable.

Grit versus Talent

☐ **Grit** means you have courage, stamina, and strength of character to persist through setbacks while pursuing your goals to their completion.

☐ **Talent** is the natural endowment of a person which appears to be an advantage.

Given the choice, a COBRA chooses grit every time. Although talent gives you a boost initially, it can make you lazy and complacent, especially if you don't have grit. After all, talent without grit is just wasted opportunity. Next time you see a professional excelling at their job, don't be a hater thinking they must have some magical talent that got them there. They don't. They are COBRAs and they have grit, and you will too by the end of the book.

Strategies to improve self discipline

• Embrace discomfort

Somewhere along the line our society has in large part become soft. Maybe it's because, for the most part, we no longer have to hunt and kill our food and can instead order groceries online. Maybe it's because our current generations haven't had to defeat Nazism. Maybe it's the fact that our children's schools no longer teach them that we live in the greatest nation in history and how it was built by men and women of backbone, courage and ingenuity. Maybe it doesn't matter. It just is.

Make no mistake. Achieving success is a battle. Fighting a battle is not always comfortable, get used to it. Embrace the discomfort and let it strengthen and harden you. Remember that steel is tempered in the fiery crucible of adversity. You do not grow in the moments of comfort and pleasure. You grow when you are challenged and out of your comfort zone. I'm a huge fan of the *Rocky* films. Rocky's manager Mickey spelled it out in *Rocky III* when he admonished Rocky about choosing material comfort over the hunger to win.

"THE WORST THING THAT HAPPENED TO YOU,
THAT CAN HAPPEN TO ANY FIGHTER: YOU GET
CIVILIZED."

-MICKEY GOLDMILL

The fire from hunger burns from the fuel of self-discipline. Self imposed discomfort builds mental toughness. Fighting your way though the discomfort defines your character. Remember, character is everything.

*   Sacrifice

Whether you deny yourself chocolate cake when everyone else enjoys a piece or you stay in on the weekend to study for that big exam, you must be willing to sacrifice. The ability to forgo instant gratification is a characteristic of self-discipline and a common denominator shared by true COBRAs.

*   *Carpe mane* - Latin for "seize the morning".

Multiple studies have supported the fact that successful individuals wake up early and own the morning. Later in the book I will teach you specific strategies to accomplish this.

*   Time management

The ability to coordinate the tasks you must accomplish with the amount of time available requires self-discipline.

*   Scheduling

Plan your schedule for the week during the previous weekend. Review your schedule for the next day. Anticipate any potential obstacles or contingencies. Create deadlines and stick to them. Create work periods/play periods, it is easier to maintain self-discipline when you divide your time into blocks of intermittent rest/reward. Using timer set periods of 20/30 or 60 minutes for work followed by a 15 minute break. Use the break to return calls, check social media and email or do push-ups.

- Environment

Your ability to maintain self-discipline can be greatly affected by your surroundings. If you're working out in the gym the sound of clanking barbells and plates comes with the territory. If you are preparing for a big presentation at work or studying for an exam that noise would be maddening. Choose your environment carefully and do your best to surround keep it orderly and neat. If you can't find solitude at home or even in your office then go to the library or invest in some good noise reducing headphones.

- Unplug and eliminate distractions.

Television and our smartphones are huge distractions. Resist the temptation to check your social media and email every five minutes. Either turn off your phone or put it in airplane mode when you must complete a task. If you don't believe this is a form of self-discipline try it for a day. Remain vigilant against Thieves of Time.

- Remove temptation

If you're focusing your self-discipline on avoiding certain things then remove the temptation. The ability to control the food we consume can present a formidable challenge. If you, like me, do battle with that demon then you need to declaw and de-fang it. It is much easier to stick to a nutrition plan when you have removed temptation. I simply do not keep junk food in my house. It's much more difficult to binge on unhealthy, fattening garbage when it's simply not readily available. Don't use your kids as an excuse. Sure kids like to eat sugary cereals and other garbage that's bad for them. If you're giving that poison to your kids, knock it off. Having it lying around your kitchen whether it's for them or for you is the same thing. Your kids and your spouse would much rather have you healthier and more active and able to spend more quality time with them than a fist full of Milk Duds or Cap'n Crunch. As an aside, I happen to love both Milk Duds and the Cap'n. All COBRAs must make sacrifices.

Here's a little tip for you. Stop watching TV punctuated with psychologically engineered commercials designed to excite your Pavlovian-response to food and incite cravings. Having worked in television for over 30 years I'm gonna share a little secret with you. Gorgeous supermodels in bathing suits generally do not stuff their face with triple-bacon-cheeseburgers dripping with barbecue sauce while twerking on a sports car. Reality check, ripped up, shirtless guys playing football on the beach generally don't consume half a case of beer on a Saturday afternoon. Both of those fantasies only happen on television.

If you struggle with over consumption of alcohol yet keep a full bar in your place then maybe it's time for a little interior decorating. It's a lot more difficult to get boozed when you don't keep alcohol in the house. If your social life revolves around power drinking sessions after work or on the weekends it may be time to find some new pursuits, like a bowling league. That way you can cut down of the liquor in between physical activity. I guarantee that anyone who is super successful and that you admire isn't shutting down TGI Fridays on a weeknight.

"STRIVE FOR PROGRESS NOT PERFECTION."
-MICHELE KANAN

• Focus on the reward

The ability to exercise self-discipline should be it's own reward. Should be, but let's be honest, sometimes it helps to keep your eye on the prize. Think about the positive results and rewards that you will achieve by sticking to the path. Focus on how great it will feel to pass a licensing exam, lose that 30 pounds you've been trying to shed for years, get that big promotion that has been alluding you or be able to frame the deed to your home because you paid it off.

There's nothing wrong with allowing yourself a reward for meeting a goal or accomplishing a series of tasks. Self-bribery can be a formidable incentivizer. I make deals with myself all the time. Like if I accomplish everything I need to do for the week I reward myself with something that I'd like to do on the weekend. Other times when I want a specific item I will tie it's purchase to the achievement of certain goals. Accountability really helps with the strategy, especially when you involve a friend or a partner or even put it out on social media that you intend to finish a specific goal. Include the date when you intend to finish and any other specifics that will hold you accountable, but avoid get discouraged by setbacks. If you miss the deadline due to unavoidable obstacles, push the deadline and carry on. Once you achieve the goal feel good about showing the world the reward you obtained for yourself. This is not meant to brag or show off but rather to inspire others to do the same.

In the course of writing this book I've had to forgo many social opportunities and good times. I have had to cloister myself alone for hours on end to complete it. Maintaining my self-discipline to write these words has been easier because I have created a positive story attached to its completion. I honestly believe that this book has the ability to change lives and help a great number of people. I committed to myself that the book would be completed and available in time for Christmas 2021. Just before New Year's people are traditionally more committed to making changes for the coming year. I told myself that not having the book available at that time would be doing a huge disservice to my readers thus creating a sense of urgency and emotion within myself that fortified my resolve and self discipline.

THE POWER OF STORY

"WHO ARE WE BUT THE STORIES WE TELL
OURSELVES, ABOUT OURSELVES AND THOSE
WE BELIEVE?"

— AUTHOR SCOTT TUROW

There are three sides to every story. My side, your side and the truth. Even the truth is subjective. Philosophical COBRA, Friedrich Nietzsche said,

"THERE ARE NO FACTS, ONLY INTERPRETATIONS."

These interpretations or stories form from individual and unique life experience. The stories you create and attach to situations, people, events and circumstances are all rationalizations, ways for you to cope and accept life when life is difficult and unfair. **SPOILER ALERT** LIFE ISN'T FAIR! Get used to it. You may be a blue belt in my dojo but I guarantee you have a black belt in the dojo of rationalizations. Trust me when I tell you that dojo's karate is a joke. One of the greatest obstacles impeding your progress are the stories you tell yourself about various experiences and people. Unfortunately the great majority of these stories work against you. People tend to cast themselves as the star in their stories. Regrettably they tend to play the victim rather than the hero. How dumb is that?

STOP taking things personally. With few exceptions it's not all about you. Imagine you are walking down a street minding your own business. An angry guy bumps into you. Being a polite COBRA you offer an apology. The man who bumped you pops off a nasty reference to your mother and caps it off by calling you a clumsy jerk. You could choose to attach the story that you are in fact a clumsy jerk and even complete strangers think so. Or you could act like the intuitive COBRA you are and recognize that the enraged gentleman probably isn't having a very good day which has nothing to do with you. Maybe his boss just fired him. Maybe his wife just left him. Maybe his boss just fired him and his wife left him for his boss. None of which has a thing to do with you. The experience which was initially classified as "negative" has now become "positive" with the attachment of a different story.

Seems logical, right? Yet humans have a never ending capacity to attach wildly inaccurate stories to events and circumstances. Almost 100% of the time these stories bear little resemblance to the truth. They are formed through the prism of our life experience. If the stories aren't an accurate representation of reality then let's at least create stories that don't perpetuate victimhood but allow you to overcome and achieve. Like this comedy routine from the legendary Danny Thomas that illustrates how creating negative stories based on presumption and not rooted in fact can wreak havoc in your life, I call them Jack Stories.

There's this traveling salesman who gets stuck one night on a lonely country road with a flat tire and no jack. So he starts walking toward a service station about a mile away, and as he walks, he talks to himself. "How much can he charge me for renting a jack?" he thinks. "One dollar, maybe two. But it's the middle of the night, so maybe there's an after-hours fee. Probably another five dollars. If he's anything like my brother-in-law, he'll figure I got no place else to go for the jack, so he's cornered the market and has me at his mercy. Ten dollars more."

He goes on walking and thinking, and the price and the anger keep rising. Finally, he gets to the service station and is greeted cheerfully by the owner: "What can I do for you, sir?" But the salesman will have none of it. "You got the nerve to talk to me, you robber," he says. "You can take your stinkin' jack and . . ."

The Lonely Cobra

The Lonely Cobra or self-abandonment is what happens when you expect someone else to take away your uncomfortable feelings or make you okay. We all feel this tinge from time to time and we eventually grow out of it. But the Lonely Cobra never evolves beyond childhood disappointments. Look, you didn't ask to be born. So it's only natural to expect your mom, who lets you tear up her body for 9 months while feeding you gourmet meals, to love you. But sometimes the fates can be cruel, and your parents didn't have this book, so one of two things happened:

1. You realized these people didn't know how to love you (It's not you, it's them), so you turned out fine and are reading this book for someone else...NOT!

2. Most likely what happened was...You attached

the wrong story by concluding there must be something wrong with you, the Lonely Cobra.

"But my parents are great, why am I the Lonely Cobra?" Get real, no human being can provide 100% love for us all the time, supermoms included. It's those lulls that the Lonely Cobra was born out of, deciding it was you not them, just because you weren't getting exactly what you thought that you should. Then starts— depression, anxiety, loneliness, and anger. Give yourself a break, you were a dumb kid, doing what kids do: either rebelling or conforming as a way to get the love/attention you thought you needed. Then you grew up and discovered something revelatory: romance. "Bingo!" The little Cobra inside you thought, "THIS person will fill in the missing love."

The Lonely Cobra's Love Life

Hey Lonely Cobra, think that finding the perfect partner will warm your cold-blooded heart and then you will always feel okay? In searching for the perfect partner, what you're really doing is looking for someone to fill those childhood lulls. Wake up! Even your parent couldn't do it for you, how do you expect a lover to do it? Lonely Cobra, no one can but you because you self-abandoned and abdicated personal responsibility for your feelings, thus transferring it to a proposed partner. That's why you feel an urgency to make sure your partner gives you what you're not giving yourself.

Subconsciously, you auto-pilot into control, and not always in the ways you might think. Control can show up in the form of being overly nice and accommodating, or in being possessive and hyper vigilant. You can control by being overly compliant and by care-taking. In each of these cases, you're trying to make sure the other person doesn't reject you. You think that by doing all these things, you won't experience all the feelings that go along with believing you're not lovable. But all good things must come to an end, this one is usually accompanied by a fiery crash because no one can maintain a persona forever in a romantic relationship because it requires intimacy which can only occur with trust and raw honesty.

Time to strike Lonely Cobra

Although your childhood may be the source of your pain and genesis of the story that you are attached to, those false beliefs are now yours. Your thoughts are colored by your beliefs and therefore cause much of your emotional state, for better or worse. You are stuck in victim mode if anger, blame, depression, or numbness are your base emotion. The only way out is a door into a different state of openness and learning. That door is open when you correct your false beliefs about past events, then develop compassion for yourself. We cannot connect with others when we're disconnected from ourselves. And we cannot share love with others when we're not loving ourselves. But when you realize that you're the only person who can truly make you feel okay, you take responsibility for your feelings. You make it your job to feel good, which in turn takes the pressure off your partner to make everything alright. As if by magic, even long-standing problems melt away as your need for control disappears.

CONTROL

"HE WHO CONTROLS OTHERS MAY
BE POWERFUL BUT HE WHO HAS
MASTERED HIS OWN EMOTIONS IS
EVEN MORE POWERFUL STILL"
-LAO TZU

Control represents one of the greatest illusions we perpetuate upon ourselves. Control is a single word oxymoron which makes those who chase it oxy-morons. Maybe it's because we are so acutely aware of our own mortality that we seek to control everything within our grasp. The simple truth is, that which we seek to control, controls us. All we have to do to confirm that we are not in control is look to our own planet whose very survival depends upon an ever dying star, our sun. It is inevitable that at some point in the distant future our sun will go supernova eventually collapsing into a black hole and devouring everything in our galaxy including our Earth. This is an inescapable fact. Still think you are in control?

The only thing in the universe that we do have control over is how we process the never-ending stream of stimuli that bombards us from the world outside and how we choose to respond with our emotions. Notice that I selected "choose" because make no mistake about it, the way you deal with a situation is a choice. Choose wisely because that choice may initiate a domino effect which next triggers the story you attach to the event. Before you even consider controlling another I suggest you gain control of yourself. I find this to be a very time consuming albeit worthwhile pursuit.

There exists a fluidity within our universe. When we fight the natural ebb and flow we tend to find ourselves out of sync with the world around us. We feel "out of control", it's not complicated. Have you ever had one of those days where you feel like a salmon swimming upstream against the current? That's because you are either out of sync with the universe or not living in consistency with your true self. Attempting to assert control over external forces is like trying to fit a round peg in a square space. It only creates frustration and anger.

Trying to control other people wreaks even more havoc, the harder we fight to exert our will over others the harder they rebel. It's human nature to recoil or resist when some attempts to impose their will upon us. More often than not, we alienate those we hope to persuade. It is equally important that you do not fall into the trap of becoming overly controlling with yourself. When taken to extremes these attempts to control lead to numerous debilitating behavioral disorders and neurosis including anorexia, bulimia and hoarding.

"BE FORMLESS... SHAPELESS. LIKE WATER.
IF YOU PUT WATER INTO A CUP, IT BECOMES THE CUP. IF YOU PUT IT INTO A TEAPOT: IT BECOMES THE TEAPOT. WATER CAN FLOW, OR IT CAN CRASH.
BE WATER, MY FRIEND..."
- BRUCE LEE

Respect the flow of the universe. Do not be rigid in your desire to control anything but yourself. Remain flexible and the universe will support you. Even the mighty oak tree snaps in a storm while the supple reed bends against the wind and survives. Besides being a martial arts legend and a level ten COBRA, Bruce Lee was a very astute philosopher. He understood the necessity of remaining flexible as a method of achieving a positive result faced with any resistance.

PERFECTION IS A MYTH

"PERFECTION IS NOT ATTAINABLE,
BUT IF WE CHASE PERFECTION
WE CAN CATCH EXCELLENCE."
-VINCE LOMBARDI

I'm sure you have someone in your life that makes everything look so easy. Their relationship is perfect, their job is always great, they seem to have life on lockdown... they've achieved perfection. On the outside it may seem that way, but perfection does not exist; not in people or situations. No situation or circumstance exists without challenges, obstacles and potential dangers. All people have flaws, we are all damaged and therefore imperfect. We all have psychic scars from past trauma. It is the quest to heal yourself and unify the lost pieces of your psyche that makes you fascinating and elevates you above the animals. COBRAs do not allow these scars to define or make us victims. Remember VICTIMS do not exist in this dojo. There is nobility in the never-ending pursuit of bettering yourself.

If anything approaches perfection it's Michelangelo's statue of David in the Galleria Dell 'Academia in Florence, Italy. If you haven't had the opportunity to see this masterpiece in person I hope that someday you will. People travel from all over the world to Florence, Italy, however, even David is far from perfect, yet there is beauty in imperfection.

David was created from a massive block of Carrara Marble (more than 6000 kilos) that came from the Apuan Alps in Northern Tuscany. "Il Gigante" had sat for decades in the Opera del Duomo, which was the works yard of the Florentine church, Santa Maria del Fiore. While exposure to the elements had taken its toll upon "Il Gigante" as the block of marble had come to be known, it was the failed sculpting attempts of two other artists which placed it's future in peril. In 1464 Agostino di Duccio drilled a hole in the block of marble where he anticipated carving the legs for a statue he was hired to create. Agostino abandoned the project leaving Il Gigante disfigured. Michelangelo was forced to work around this imperfection when creating David. His ability to create a masterpiece from such imperfect origins should serve as inspiration for all of us. While we are clearly imperfect that does not mean that we too cannot become a masterpiece. Legend has it that when asked how he created the nearly perfect statue of David, Michelangelo replied "I saw the angel in the marble and carved until I set him free." The essence of David already existed within Il Gigante. He took the dedication and genius of Michelangelo to release him from his marble prison. Conversely you are chipping away at the imperfect blocks of fear and doubt imprisoning your inner masterpiece.

In addition to David's imperfect origins, the finished product is also imperfect. There is a minor flaw between David's right scapula and spine. He is missing a muscle. Some art historians speculate that young Michelangelo did this intentionally. Believing himself not yet as talented as many of his more mature peers, he embedded the imperfection as a demonstration of his humility. Still others believe the missing muscle was a result of an imperfection in Il Gigante. Even a masterpiece has flaws.

PATIENCE

"YOU GET THE CHICKEN BY HATCHING
THE EGG, NOT BY SMASHING IT
OPEN."
- ARNOLD GLASOW

Patience is the ability to stay calm while you're waiting for an outcome that you need or want. It's a spectrum from every day hassles to life long hardships. It requires delaying gratification while focusing on the actions necessary to achieve a desired goal without having an outburst. Different challenges require different levels of patience. While it's frustrating to wait in line at the grocery store for some joker to write a personal check for a carton of milk, in fact, it doesn't require the patience of Job, or at least it shouldn't. On a scale of 1 to 10 that probably comes in at about a four. Conversely, a young military spouse waiting for their significant other to return home from a tour of duty in a far away deployment or worse yet, war, would definitely merit a ten on that scale. Embarking upon significant weight loss at least in my experience comes in around an eight. Perseverance, determination and focus are required to overcome a serious obstacle in life or achieve a long term goal. You will need to keep your emotions in check throughout the journey. Emotions can range from eagerness to get it done to anger at the frustrations you encounter, a COBRA doesn't become demotivated. There is an overlap with self-discipline when it comes to long term desires. We are going to focus on immediate situations that provoke impatience.

Losing your patience manifests physically resulting in fast breathing, muscle tension, hand clenching and feet jiggling in addition to the classic irritability, anger, anxiety, nervousness or outburst. You may make snap decisions in your rush to just get it over with. Imagine, for instance, that you encounter a new employee trying to learn in the job. She politely, yet cluelessly asks for some information. You're already late, you can feel your body getting tense, and you're starting to get angry. Suddenly, you lose it and a level 9 meltdown ensues hurling some regrettably choice venomous words. You can tell that the new guy is shocked and upset by your helpful suggestion to die uncomfortably, but it's beyond your control. People are frustrating, slow learners, slow reactors, hard to understand, unreasonable, have annoying bad habits and generally just bug. But losing your patience with them will not change that fact. It will only exacerbate your frustration and their being flustered because almost no one is their best when they are under duress. We all lose our patience, but in doing so frequently or inappropriately can harm your reputation, damage your relationships, increase stress, or escalate a difficult situation. Not very COBRA.

Being patient has it's benefits, you'll be viewed as a cool cucumber by those around you. Acting with patience requires effectively managing anxiety, enduring discomfort and restlessness while maintaining balance in anticipation of achieving a specific result. You'll be a better team member, not to mention, more focused and productive. Venom is weapon that is a privilege to use, so use yours sparingly and wisely. If you're often impatient, people will view you as arrogant, insensitive and impulsive believing you don't care enough to give them your time. Co-workers will view you as a poor decision maker, because you make snap judgments or interrupt people. If you get a reputation for having poor people skills and a bad temper, people will deliberately avoid working with you. Not surprising, impatient people will not make the employee of the month nor get a key to the executive lavatory.

However, being patient doesn't mean you should be a softie suffering in silence, it's OK to speak your mind when someone wastes your time deliberately. But temper your reaction to fit the situation. A COBRA flares it's hood only when provoked and strikes only when threatened. The key to everything is patience.

I WANT IT ALL. I WANT IT ALL. I WANT IT ALL. AND I WANT IT NOW.
-FREDDY MERCURY, QUEEN

"I don't have patience" is a crap excuse used by white belts. Every one has patience when they want to, usually when their WHY is powerful enough, it's just wanting to use it that's the problem. Patience does not have an on/off switch, rather it's tethered to frustration. It's that "heat" creeping up your neck when you feel that you are being ignored. Remember in the Bugs Bunny cartoons when Elmer Fudd's face would fill up with red? That was him losing his patience. Confession time. Your Sensei has not always been the paragon of discipline and patience. Confession number two. Your Sensei still struggles with discipline and patience. COBRAs are human and therefore not perfect. Remember, life is a marathon (if you are lucky) and not a fifty-yard dash. COBRAs fight the good fight and DO NOT QUIT.

How do I increase my patience, Sensei?

Like anything else, patience requires training. You must learn to identify feelings and their triggers, regulate your emotions, and empathize with others. Listening skills and empathy are vital when you're dealing with difficult people. In just a short time, you will feel more patient toward the trying people in your life, feel less depressed, and experience higher levels of positive emotions. Here are a few of the tactics I use to achieve my goals which generally requires... wait for it... patience.

- HALT Hungry, Angry, Lonely, Tired. These are powerful feelings which can easily trigger frustration, irritability and lack of patience. Remember kindergarten? Snack time/nap time may be just the ticket.

- When you feel impatient, it's important to get out of this damaging frame of mind as quickly as possible. Force yourself to slow down, speak and move more slowly, I promise your version of speed is not in sync with your audience's. Any change in speed will translate as calm. Acting patient often makes you feel more patient, so fake it til you make it. Meditation works. Back to kindergarten, sometimes you have to give yourself a time out.

- Re-frame your thinking before your impatience grows. Recognize the temporary nature by challenging your hasty, negative assumptions with a more positive spin. Don't let frustration get the better of you by being so attached to the immediacy of reacting. Simply put, cool your jets.

- When pursuing a goal or faced with a task that requires patience, Pre-game it. Prior to the task, write down the desired outcome, include the positive and negatives of completing or not completing the task. Embrace the suck by listing potential obstacles or pitfalls that you may face and how you can address them. Keep this list with you and refer to it frequently. Now you have clarity about your *WHY*. This will drive, motivate and remind you why you're in the fight so that you can keep your cool.

- You can choose to be patient or not. Remember the second pillar that comprises the *Way of the COBRA*: optimization.

COBRAs chose appropriate and best reactions. at that moment. If the best and most appropriate reaction isn't possible then it's time to disengage and reevaluate. Stay focused on the goal to override your feelings of frustration.

- Don't underestimate the power of self bribery to keep yourself on track. Example: If you do not interrupt during the explanation of the problem, then give yourself an extra ten minutes of free time.

Warning:

If you find yourself becoming more impatient or having outbursts that are prolonged or unrelated, it may be a sign of underlying problems such as stress, exhaustion or burnout. If you think this may apply to you, seek advice from a qualified health professional. I'm giving general advice to improve, a pro will give you treatment tailored specifically to you and your situation.

GREEN BELT

DEFINE YOUR SUCCESS

"Success usually comes to those who are too busy to be looking for it."

-Henry David Thoreau

A few years ago I found myself in a dark place that you may identify with. After achieving some notable success in my life, I faced down some tough challenges and experienced some epic failures. To make matters worse I was 30 pounds overweight, unemployed with no prospects of work and running into old demons more frequently than I'd like to admit. In short, I needed a good swift kick in the ass because I had given up. Definitely not the behavior of a COBRA.

I'm not sure when it happened, probably after suffering too many negative consequences, but I made the decision to start doing things differently. I knew it was time for me to save myself by unleashing my inner badass. I decided there was no more of this "waiting for my ship to come in" crap; I was going to build the damn ship. I just had to figure out how. I was faced with a glaring question when I looked at my reflection in the mirror: What next? Winston Churchill said it best, (if you haven't figured it out yet, that boozy, old, English COBRA holds a special place in my heart.)

"THOSE WHO DON'T LEARN FROM HISTORY
ARE DOOMED TO REPEAT IT"

Which led me to think about the times in my life when I was really in the zone, when I felt unstoppable. Those moments when I just knew, without any empirical evidence, that I was going to succeed at whatever I set out to do. I made a list of all of my successes and how I achieved them. Because hindsight is 20/20, I was able to pinpoint what was the secret of my success. In those periods of my life I was clear about what it meant to succeed and what I needed to do to achieve it. In other words, my success was defined.

You can't embark on a successful journey without knowing your intended destination. In this case success is the destination. It's obvious when you think about it, how can you achieve success/victory if you don't know where the finish line is? But hold on... you must define what success means to you. Not my definition of success, not your parents' definition and not the definition of success foisted on us through television and social media. You must form in your mind a clearly defined vision of what it would mean for you to be successful.

It certainly doesn't look like anyone else's version of success or at least it shouldn't... Remember, your success is your own personal definition of success. Comparing it to other people's success is a waste of time because only you know what makes you happy. You will know when you are living up to it and when you are falling short. So stop comparing your current position with the perceived success of others. I say perceived because frequently the image that people put out into the world has very little to do with reality and looks more like the airbrushed covers of fashion magazines that set completely unrealistic goals for men and women alike. Trust me, I work in Hollywood I know what I'm talking about. My Uncle Geoffrey, an O.G. COBRA has a very wise saying:

"THINGS AREN'T ALWAYS AS THEY SEEM.
SKIM MILK MASQUERADES AS CREAM"

That's especially true in social media feeds featuring a parade of toys and backdrops that portray a high-end lifestyle which are usually photoshopped or staged. Their reality rarely matches the success they portray. Besides, if financial success and material possessions were to serve as the only benchmarks of achievement then a spectacular percentage of the population would find themselves deemed failures. The English band, The Verve, captures the tragic insanity that has become the motivating force for so many of us.

"IT'S A BITTERSWEET SYMPHONY THIS
LIFE. TRYIN' TO MAKE ENDS MEET. YOU'RE
A SLAVE TO THE MONEY THEN YOU DIE."

Your life must be more than the sum total of your possessions. You are not your home, your car or your job. No matter how much you think your work defines you. Character is what defines us. I have never been in military combat. I'm sure some of you have had that unique experience. I thank you for your service. I would never presuppose to understand what that must be like. I can say that if I were facing an enemy on the field of battle, the last thing I would care about is that person's socioeconomic status and the possessions they had or didn't have. You know what I would care about? THEIR CHARACTER! Will this individual next to me fight until death or victory? Will they have my back even at the expense of their own?

Success comes in many shapes and sizes. A COBRA remains open to recognizing non-traditional success in themselves and others. A man who spends his entire life toiling as a janitor would probably not be considered "successful" by most of society. What if, however, that same man diligently saved his honest and hard-earned wages and ultimately put his daughter through medical school? What if she went on to become a brilliant research scientist saving countless lives? Wouldn't we then agree that this man epitomizes the American dream and represents a very special type of success?

Don't allow yourself to fall into the trap of defining success in yourself or others by superficial standards. Let character guide the path to YOUR success. Stop envying other people's lives. Remember:

OTHER PEOPLE'S SUCCESS IS NOT YOUR FAILURE

Allow their success to inspire you, to motivate, and drive you to accomplishing your goals and achieve your success that is yours and yours alone. Examine the success of those individuals you admire. Look for clues. Ask yourself how they achieved success and what you may learn from their journey. Chances are they trained to get to where they are instead of just figuring it out on the fly. The difference is like a very good bar-room brawler versus a highly trained professional boxer. Nine out of ten times the boxer will wipe the floor with the brawler because consistently working with other professionals who push you and force you to bring your A-game makes for a formidable competitor whether it's boxing or acting.

My parents raised me to appreciate education and understand the doors that it opened. When I first moved to Los Angeles to pursue my career in acting, I knew that in order to have any realistic chance at succeeding as a professional actor I had to acquire a very specific, difficult and expensive skill set. I was just one of many young actors from small-town USA looking to parlay youthful good looks and untrained charisma into legitimate, trained talent and a career in film and television.

Besides learning acting technique, character analysis, script analysis and about a hundred other things, I needed to face some old ghosts. I needed to learn how to break down the emotional walls that I created to protect me from years of bullying as a young kid. I had to access my internal vulnerability. In the acting game naked, honest emotions are the silk required to spin gold that glitters in Tinseltown.

So I began studying with the late Roy London, universally

considered one of the greatest acting teachers of his time. He was demanding, critical, and brutally honest. He also possessed a keen intellect allowing him to intuitively understand the essence of a scene and to convey that to his students. This made him one of the best. He was indeed a COBRA. This also made his class one of the most respected and difficult to join. I was very green but I was very determined. Between expensive private coaching, the occasional work on a professional sets and real life experience in the "city of lost angels" I slowly began to improve. As hard as I worked there were others who had been there longer, had way more professional experience, and if I'm being honest had a better work ethic. Something in retrospect that I wish I had cultivated at a much younger age and I've had to learn as an adult through banging my head against a wall until I found a better way. Now you will benefit from the wisdom I learned from my trial and error as you become a COBRA.

One of the other young actors in my class was from Missouri. He was both incredibly handsome and highly talented, his name was Brad Pitt. In the beginning we frequently auditioned against each other and one time I actually beat him out of a part for a television show called Baby Boom starring Kate Jackson from the original Charlie's Angels series. On another occasion I remember leaving an audition for the film Days of Thunder. To say that the audition hadn't been stellar would probably be an understatement. Although I was growing as an actor I had a very long way to go. As I made my way into the parking lot I remember seeing Brad sitting on the curb alone. He had auditioned just before me. I smiled at him and asked "How'd it go?" He cracked his now famous sideways smile. I'm not exactly sure now what he said but it didn't seem like he set the room on fire either. Apparently both of us were right because Carey Elwes wound up winning the role to play Tom Cruise's rival, Russ Wheeler driving the number 51 Exxon Chevrolet. Loved that film. It goes without saying that Cruise is a COBRA as is Brad.

Obviously my career and Brad Pitt's career have taken wildly different paths. If I were to compare my success with Brad's success I would find myself in a perpetual state of envy, dissatisfaction, and unhappiness. Instead I'm inspired by his success and honestly very happy for him because he's a good guy. Hell, I'll say it with confidence; I'm a fan. We all have our own internal compass that lets us know when we're moving in the right direction toward our personal definition of success, it's called confidence. Confidence comes from knowing that you are successful and the only way to know success is to design it for yourself. Let's build some confidence by doing an exercise.

1. Write down your definition of success.

Take as much time as necessary and create the most detailed version of your personal success into succinct, clear and unambiguous bullet points. But do it right now! What would have to occur for you to consider yourself successful? Abundant health, vibrant and passionate love, financial freedom, respect, a yellow Lamborghini? For me, I think about what I have to manifest to feel truly successful. I already married the girl of my dreams, have a loving, supportive family, and, at least for the moment, a roof over my head, a car and a few bucks in my savings account. But, I've always had the ability to dream big so I'm not done succeeding yet.

Here's my list from a few years ago :

- I will create, star in and sell my television show, *STUDiO CiTY*
- I will spend quality time with my wife.
- I will lose thirty-five pounds.
- I will finish my book, *SUCCESS FACTORx*
- I will secure a publishing deal.
- I will launch *SUCCESS FACTORx* at the Barnes and Noble flagship store at the Grove in Los Angeles to a star-studded audience.

I used to walk by that store all the time seeing the banners advertising authors and celebrities who were coming to do book signings. It stabbed at me every single time because my first book *The Modern Gentleman; Cooking and Entertaining with Sean Kanan* was not launched in that store nor was it featured there, but it was on the shelf. Notice when I created my list that I didn't write " I want to do" or "I need to do" or "I'm going to try to do". This is important, each goal is written as a positive statement of fact. When a COBRA gives their word, they keep it, especially to themselves.

****SHAMELESS PLUG:****
It's a quick read if you want to fine-tune your game...

www.SeanKananTheModernGentleman.com

2. Organize your list in order of importance to you.
Remember, you are the author of your success, so you must prioritize what's most important to you. Make sure that you are specific with your list and be realistic about what's important to you versus what's going to help you realize your goals.

3. Now take a picture of that list with your phone.
Congratulations! You just created your new screensaver. Put it on your phone. NOW! Feeling the confidence growing? Great, now let's get back to me. Not the badass COBRA I am now but the overweight, unemployed and unfocused guy from that period in time a few years ago, who now had a list. Having clearly identified what my success would look like, I was ready for the next step and so are you.

DEFINE YOUR WHY

"HE WHO HAS A WHY
CAN ENDURE ANY HOW."
-FREDERICK NIETZSCHE

When the going gets tough (and believe me it will), you need to know why you're doing what you're doing. Why you're struggling through times of difficulty and frustration. What makes it all worth it when you're not getting the accolades or hearing the crowd cheer or pulling in the big paycheck or even seeing a light at the end of the tunnel. That driving reason that gets you out of bed and keeps you on the path to achieving your goals and reaching your success is called your *Why*. You must identify your *Why*. During the darkest times your *Why* will fuel you, ignite the fire in your belly, remind you that you've got more in the tank and to keep going. Cue the *Rocky* theme music.

+ Your *Why* will push you to do one more rep when you have nothing left.

+ Your *Why* will wake you up in the morning while the rest of the world hits the snooze button.

+ Your *Why* will ensure that your partner never looks at you with silent regret.

Now that you know what a *Why* is, we must pinpoint yours. If you fail to clarify your *Why*, you **may** succeed but you won't be able to continue winning and COBRAs don't leave anything to chance, so take a minute and have a conversation with yourself, I do it all the time. Maybe your WHY is to silence the naysayers. Those little-brains who thought that you didn't have what it takes, that you'd never make it- usually because they allowed their fears to overtake them and consume their dreams. When all the hateful doubters circle you like vultures eying a wounded animal, your *Why* will give you the strength to ignore, carry on and win.

For as long as I can remember I have struggled with my weight. As a chubby 12-year-old I implored my mother to take me to Weight Watchers. This began what has been a lifelong kumite with the refrigerator. I've had periods in my life *where I've experienced great success losing weight and other times, well, not so much. When I made the conscious decision to lose the thirty-five pounds aka the spare tire around my chin and waist that I had acquired like a keepsake on my vacation from the gym and good behavior, I recognized that it would not happen overnight and would indeed require the "P" word, patience. It was not only going to take a change in lifestyle but would necessitate refining a personality trait, patience, that has frequently been in short supply in my wheelhouse. What I have not shared with you is the tragic news that I have suffered my entire life with "ain't-got-no-patience-itis." As a general rule, weight loss never occurs as quickly as we would like. In my experience it takes at least a month before I start recognizing positive signs and takes at least twice that long before friends and loved ones take notice. Losing excess weight for me had many potential upsides however my strongest WHY was my love for acting. I knew that not losing the weight would be an obstacle precluding me from getting hired. The thought of not being able to do what I love was a powerful WHY. Conversely the possibility of new and exciting professional opportunities was an effective motivator.*

Haters will attribute your success to external forces like you had greater opportunity and advantages, or even luck. They are also the first to smile when you get knocked down claiming you never had what it took in the first place. Little do they know COBRAs are fueled by obstacles, they ignite a catalytic combustion that screams "I WON'T QUIT!" Ignore their insults and ridicule because COBRAs always prove them wrong.

DON'T SHUT 'EM OUT; LET 'EM DRIVE YOU.

Doubters are waiting for you to stumble so they can take what you have built. The reflection of your success doesn't just reflect back at them, it scorches them. Maybe that will trigger them to become a COBRA and stop trying to steal your thunder. Who knows, you may even become their Sensei... this is the dojo of infinite possibilities.

- While you are partying someone is training.
- While you are sleeping, someone is grinding.
- While you are complaining someone is planning.

Maybe your *Why* is that you never want to look into the faces of those who depend upon you, who love you, and see disappointment because you weren't able to take care of them. Maybe you're *Why* developed because you grew up in poverty. It could be that you had to watch one or both of your parents work multiple jobs just to put food on the table and pay the rent. You watched as it ran them into the ground just a little more with each passing day. It compromised the quality of your childhood and shaped the opportunities presented to you. You vowed you wouldn't ever lack the money or resources, to provide for yourself and your family.

Your *Why* can also be motivated by a person. Maybe you made a promise to honor a dying relative by living a fulfilling life. Maybe you promised yourself that you would never become like someone from your past. You and only you can get in touch with your *Why*.

COMPLAINING MANIFESTS BAD RESULTS

For me, my *Why* is to inspire the world starting with the people I love and who love me. I never want to see the look on my wife's face that says I have let her down and I'm not living up to my potential. I never want to see that look of disappointment in the eyes of my family. Lastly, I never want to look in the mirror and feel that I have let myself down because I have squandered my one opportunity to inspire all of you and the world to live your best life. The pain associated with that drives me. That is my *Why*.

Once you have zeroed in on your *Why* things become much more clear. All of your efforts become turbo charged. Defining your purpose or *Why* for some people is simple. For others it requires some soul searching. Here are a few questions for you.

- What are your innate strengths and talents?
- What are your core values?
- What brings you joy?
- What matters most to you?

Visualize the possibilities. What would your life look like if you sprang out of bed every morning, overflowing with passion and purpose? What would that feel like? How would it positively affect your relationships? Would it make you a better person, a better spouse, a better parent, a better leader? How would it improve your opportunities to inspire those around?

Create a tangible representation of your *Why*? For me it is my wedding band which symbolizes the most important commitment in my life and the love in my heart. It can be anything; a charm, a religious symbol, a photo or a tattoo. Carry it with you as a constant reminder of what it is that inspires and drives you to accomplish your goals and fulfill your destiny. So many people fail because they lose focus or change their mind or it's out-of-sight-out-of-mind. This COBRA move will force you to stick with it until you succeed.

CLARIFY YOUR GOALS

"VICTORIOUS WARRIORS WIN FIRST
THEN GO TO WAR,

WHILE DEFEATED WARRIORS GO TO
WAR FIRST THEN SEEK TO WIN."
-SUN TZU

I know that you can't throw a spinning back kick without hitting someone or something talking about goals, what they are and the importance of setting them. So I'm not going to bore you with an explanation or even a definition. This dojo is about success not micro-managing. But if you are in the .01% of people who don't know how to use a seatbelt or know what a goal is, the internet will be happy to provide it for you. Besides, the last two sections basically set your goals to success and mapped out your reason for reaching them. So let's focus on setting COBRA goals as a plan of attack. Time for the rubber to meet the road and shift into action.

1. Grab a pen and five sheets of paper.

No, you can't do this on your laptop. It's a proven fact that handwriting, (using a pen and paper), creates a stronger connection in your brain than typing. Experts agree that because handwriting forces you to slow down to form the letters, your brain gives more attention to what is being written and you are able to memorize it faster. COBRAs are all about integrating proven methods to achieve success. As I'm write this... I realize newer tablets have handwriting recognition... so I leave it up to your COBRA discretion.

"A DREAM WRITTEN DOWN WITH A DATE
BECOMES A GOAL. A GOAL BROKEN DOWN
INTO STEPS BECOMES A PLAN. A PLAN
BACKED BY ACTION MAKES YOUR DREAMS
COME TRUE."

That's a quote by Greg Reid - renowned business and wealth

expert. Pretty smart guy, obviously a COBRA. His words are very fitting for how you will change your life in five key steps. Commit to taking positive action and you will be on your way to achieving success. Your inner badass will be proud.

2. Write each word, from the box below, on the top of each paper. You will need the whole sheet.

Use your pen and five sheets of paper or tablet for this exercise. (We're using a new acronym for COBRA just in this exercise.)

$ **Consider**
$ **Organize**
$ **Begin**
$ **Review**
$ **Adjust**

→ **CONSIDER**

Time to face the music and get real. COBRAs hate fires but recognize that they are a part of life's uncertainty. Fires are those issues that pose immediate danger and must be extinguished immediately or they will explode, threatening your balance. Consider anything in your life that constitutes an immediate threat or danger to block your success in achieving your goals. Take stock of your current situation before designing a strategy for the future. Focusing on success to the exclusion of your problems is the fastest way to fail. Be honest, fearless and ruthless with yourself. Long story short, deal with immediate threats before long term goals.

WHEN YOU START FROM THE BOTTOM, YOU
CAN'T FAIL

3. Under CONSIDER, list any life issues requiring immediate attention.

List these in order of importance. Do you have outstanding bills, obligations, academic or work related assignments? Do you have unpaid citations? Does your car need repairs? Do you have medical issues? Are you facing eviction? Do you have child support owed? Feel free to anticipate any possible upcoming obstacles as well, like, holiday spending or seasonal work.

4. List three separate and distinct actions you can take to improve or resolve the situation.

This is what I like to call the BITE-SIZE ATTACK. It comes from the old joke "how does a cobra eat an elephant?" Answer : one bite at a time. This has saved me from quitting more than I care to admit. I turn tasks into bite-size games like, have you ever looked at your messy bedroom and thought, 'I don't even know where to begin'? I apply bite-size attack by choosing 5 things to put away (I'll be honest, it's usually whatever is blocking the TV) Then I take a break and distract myself with something super important, like scrolling through my feed... yes that was sarcasm. Then it's 5 more and on and on until it's done. Each time I wanna quit, I remember my *why* : who you are is where you are and if your living environment is not tidy, your mind will not be either. Besides, should you have company in your bedroom... you want the focus to be on you, not the mess.

EXAMPLE- You owe some money or have fallen behind in payments. Write down exactly what you owe for each creditor, placing any past due accounts at the top, then the highest interest rates first to the lowest. Contact each of your creditors and ask if they would be willing to lower your interest payments and/or offer a debt relief program. Make sure to get everything in writing before agreeing to anything and ask as many questions as you need to in order to make the best decision for you. Keep in mind that there may be consequences to your credit score so be a COBRA and ask questions about the outcome. The immediate goal is to reduce the monthly debt burden you are carrying while protecting and raising your credit score. You would be amazed at how some creditors will work with you in good faith if they see that you are genuinely concerned with your credit and either repairing negative debt history or working to protect your accounts from becoming delinquent. You may have to sacrifice for a while, but your *why* will help you stay on track.

EXAMPLE- You have a medical condition that requires treatment. This is a problem that can not be solved with patience, no pun intended. Presumably lack of money is what has kept you from taking care of it or maybe you are afraid of going to the doctor.

COBRAs recognize that situations are never perfect so you play the hand you're dealt. You can replace money, but not your health. Determine the optimum course of action with a medical professional, I can promise you it is not playing video games on your couch. Get all the information you can so that you can make an informed decision about how to proceed. Half the stress is not knowing. Once you know what you are dealing with, there are tons of support groups to help you through both emotionally and financially. But you must remember your *why* in order to take this step, if you can't do it for you.

EXAMPLE - *Your relationship is in trouble or falling apart.*
COBRAs love fiercely so this is a tough one. But the best plan of action is to communicate. That's right, rip the bandage off and ask the hard questions. Make a list of your issues, don't be petty! Put the list away for a day or so and reread it as if it was given to you. Does it sound snarky? Re-word it into neutral action words instead of commentary. Your goal is understanding and compromise, not open mic night. Once you have your list, propose a time to talk. It sets the tone for it to be a discussion instead of an ambush. If you are unable to control your emotions, sometimes it's better to discuss over text. Although COBRAs look their opponents in the eye, they know when to use other tools available to achieve the best result. You can even handwrite a letter... unless your handwriting is like mine... then type and print. Use any way available to get the issues discussed while making both of your heard and understood. That is your goal. If your request to communicate is denied or ignored, that may be your answer and you will have to make some tough decisions. If it is the end, COBRAs handle defeat with grace and poise not vengeance and vitriol because this dojo is about looking to the future not making a mess in the moment.

→ ORGANIZATION

Organization is imperative for reaching any goals and achieving success. It facilitates better communication, expedites tasks, reduces wasted time, increases productivity, protects your credit score, and as an added bonus it reduces stress. Less stress, less Cortisol which is a hormone that inhibits weight loss, causes hair thinning, acne and about a dozen other little treats that you don't want. Who knew getting organized can actually help you lose weight? Remember that everything is interconnected. Organization will increase your self confidence and even enhance your personal relationships. Organization will prevent you from missing appointments or being that person who appears not to respect other people's time because you're always running late. "I couldn't find my keys" is not something employers like to hear.

Before organizing the six key areas of your life you need to organize your living space. Your home is your personal dojo. It must remain clean and orderly. A disorderly dojo is an outward manifestation of a disorderly head-space. You have chosen to unleash your inner badass, a new and vastly improved you, let your living space reflect that.

If you are one of those individuals living in clutter and even worse a general lack of cleanliness you need to sanitize, clean and organize your dojo. If you are a garden variety slob then it's time to grow up. If your dojo is overrun by messy little white belts then it's time to teach those little COBRAs how to respect their space through organization and order. I promise you will feel a renewed sense of self esteem. Throw on your favorite music and make with the wax on wax off. If that doesn't work, remember the BITE-SIZE ATTACK. Take the entire day if necessary to bring order to chaos. Streamline.

If you have adequate space including just a small corner of an apartment make that area into an office. From now on this is where you put mail, outgoing correspondence, etc. Create stations around your home to set you up for success. We've all heard of Retail Therapy, but we aren't agreed on the definition. The COBRA definition is to reward your effort with a purchase, not browse around a store buying stuff to make yourself feel better. Make your home resemble a retail store. (Hint: they design them in a way to make you feel relaxed so you open your wallet) Everything is organized and displayed where you can find it. How much time would that save?

If you have clothes you no longer wear or if they no longer fit you try to make some fast cash on a sales app or donate them. Any piece of paper that you have not looked at for over eight weeks gets tossed. Your chairs should not be covered in laundry nor are they a jacket rack. If you have anxiety over any of these purging suggestions, you may be a hoarder. If you are a hoarder seek help and for Pete's sake, CLEAN THAT CAT BOX!!! DO NOT PROCEED UNTIL YOU HAVE FINISHED CLEANING, STREAMLINING and ORGANIZING YOUR DOJO.

Now that you have finished take a nice deep breath and look around you. Doesn't that look great and make you feel good? NOW KEEP IT THAT WAY! Now you are prepared to create the battle plan which will guide you to success. Grab your papers and pen.

ORGANIZATION

	30 DAYS	1 YEAR	3 YEARS	5 YEARS
PHYSICAL				
GOALS				
ACTIONS				
OBSTACLES				
SOLUTIONS				
EMOTIONAL				
GOALS				
ACTIONS				
OBSTACLES				
SOLUTIONS				
MENTAL				
GOALS				
ACTIONS				
OBSTACLES				
SOLUTIONS				
FINANCIAL				
GOALS				
ACTIONS				
OBSTACLES				
SOLUTIONS				
SPIRITUAL				
GOALS				
ACTIONS				
OBSTACLES				
SOLUTIONS				
CREATIVE				
GOALS				
ACTIONS				
OBSTACLES				
SOLUTIONS				

5. Under ORGANIZATION, write :
"30 DAYS", "1 YEAR", "3 YEARS" and "5 YEARS."

You can fold the paper into four columns is that helps. The idea is to be able to add the following rows vertically :

- PHYSICAL
- EMOTIONAL
- MENTAL
- FINANCIAL
- SPIRITUAL
- CREATIVE

Under each category you will create four subcategories consisting of goals, actions, obstacles and optimal solutions.
(See the example to the left or get a template download from www.WAYoftheCOBRA.com) Let's turn our attention to the important stuff, filling in your chart. You will find the meaning of the headings on the next pages. Keep in mind that you will need to select a 30 day goal, a 1 year goal, 3 year goal and a 5 year goal for each topic and sub-topic.

PHYSICAL

Physical well-being gives you the greatest chance to live your longest life which in turn gives you the opportunity to affect the most change. There are three aspects to physical well-being: Activity, Diet, and Sleep, you must balance all three. Physical conditioning and health contribute largely to living a vibrant life well into our senior years, not to mention eliminate anxiety and other negative feelings you may have. Bottom line: If you are weak, fatigued and have an unhealthy diet your chance of reaching your goals and achieving success is greatly diminished.

A. **Fitness and conditioning** - Commit to exercising three times a week.

- OBSTACLE: I can't afford a gym membership.

- DEFENSE: Go to the track at the local high school, take a thirty-minute walk or do some push-ups. As a matter of fact, put down this book and give me fifteen push-ups. NOW.

B. Weight management and nutrition - Remove all junk food from your cupboards and cease eating any fast food. Weigh yourself every morning and keep a log of my progress. Eat for nutrition not entertainment and satiety.

- OBSTACLE: I work so much and only have a thirty minute lunch break.

- DEFENSE: Take several hours over the weekend to purchase your food for the week and then do meal preparation twice a week. Bring your lunch in reusable plastic ware. You will save money in the long run and you can eat healthy nourishing food instead of empty calories.

C. Sleep hygiene - Commit to eight hours of sleep and not return to the bed once awake.

- OBSTACLE: I have difficulty falling asleep.
- DEFENSE: Drink some chamomile tea, take some melatonin and Valerian Root, select a sleep hypnosis program on the internet. They are free and work. Make sure your room is dark when you are going to sleep and in the morning allow the light to come into the room. This helps reset your circadian rhythm.

D. External Appearance - Commit to more personal hygiene.

- OBSTACLES: There shouldn't be any. There's no excuse for not having good personal hygiene.

EMOTIONAL

Emotional well-being allows us to have a healthy relationship with our thoughts, desires and aspirations. It is largely derived from living in the present not regretting the past nor fearing the future. Cobras frequently shed their skin allowing beautiful, new skin to emerge; COBRAs are human and make mistakes. Forgiving yourself is the way that we shed the "skin" of our past. In this dojo, we try to understand the mistakes of others and offer them forgiveness.

1. I agree to forgive myself for something I deeply regret and which I am embarrassed.

2. Write for five minutes in a journal every morning. Do not censor or judge yourself or what appears on the page.

3. I will begin therapy to deal with past trauma which still burdens me.

- OBSTACLES: I cannot afford therapy. I am not ready to engage in therapy.

- DEFENSE: I will investigate books, support groups or online sites that offer help for my specific issue.

MENTAL

Enriching your mind and constantly challenging yourself serves as gymnastics for the brain. In this dojo, we always remain the student. Forcing your mind to work in new ways helps with critical thinking, problem-solving and creativity. Everything is interconnected.
1. Watch one documentary a week for thirty days.
2. Read a subject completely outside my wheelhouse
3. Begin learning a new language.

- OBSTACLES: Learn a language, but I don't know where to start.

- DEFENSE: Almost every library has a language arts section where you can check out free books, videos and audio aids. YouTube and Duolingo are full of online language lessons. There are numerous free apps you can download to your smart phone. Commit to studying twenty minutes three times a week.

FINANCIAL

Money doesn't create happiness but it certainly makes life easier when you're unhappy. Money provides options and security that COBRAs need to thrive. Money is not the root of all evil; the love of money is the root of all evil according to The Apostle

Paul. Having a healthy relationship with money and a reasonable understanding of finance and investment is a necessity. If you are struggling financially right now, you are not alone; the world is struggling financially. You may be thinking, "I do not have a dollar to spare, in fact I'm in debt with no way out, why do I need to know about investments?" Simple, if you don't know about it you have zero chance of obtaining it. The world of finance will sharpen your focus on your success and expose you to new opportunities. Your inner badass will know what to do.

1. Open an online brokerage account with $100.00.
2. Spend one hour a week learning how real estate, credit markets and equities function.
3. Create a budget.
4. Make sure you have apps for all of your credit card and banking institutions.
5. Obtain life insurance.

- OBSTACLES: I don't need to learn about finances. Anyone I've ever met that had money must've stepped on somebody to get there. I don't wanna be that guy.

- DEFENSE: I'm going to learn everything I can about finances so that I can increase my financial power in order to help more people and make positive change in the world.

SPIRITUALITY

It has been said that religion is for those who are afraid of hell, and spirituality is for those who have been there. Spirituality helps us to explore life's bigger questions in order to help us make sense of ourselves. It allows us to feel connected to our higher power, to those with whom we share this world and ourselves. COBRAs use it to handle life's challenges in an ethical and moral way.

1. If you believe in a higher power, then you should communicate daily.
2. Meditate each day.
3. Start each day saying out loud five reasons you are grateful.
4. Donate time to a charitable organization.

5. Spend time in nature without listening to music or speaking.

- OBSTACLES: I'm not religious. I don't know if I believe in God.

- DEFENSE: I will work to realize my authentic self. I will seek to find connection with others and the world around me. I will do this with random acts of kindness.

CREATIVITY

"CREATIVITY IS INTELLIGENCE HAVING FUN."
-ALBERT EINSTEIN

Imagination is the fuel for creativity. Inspiration nourishes the imagination. Nurturing both are vitally important to live a full, well-rounded life and achieve true success. Music, art, film, literature, architecture, travel and different cultures are all great sources for inspiration for COBRAs. Creativity allows us to transform esoteric thoughts and human emotion. As a mathematician Albert Einstein was one of the most concrete thinkers in history yet his ability to think creatively led him to discover the earth-shattering theory of relativity. He used to imagine what it would be like to ride on a beam of light as it extended out into the universe. You can feed your creativity if you:

1. Listen to a jazz album.
2. Visit a museum.
3. Go on a walking tour of your city.
4. Watch a foreign film.

- OBSTACLES: I'm a concrete, logical thinker, I don't need creativity to do my job.

- DEFENSE: I will challenge myself to explore non-traditional and creative options that can be integrated with tried and true logic.

Goals and **actions** should be as specific. If you have always wanted to visit the Sistine Chapel do not write that you want to go to Europe. The more powerful the image the more likely you will work to make it a reality. Some people believe that goals should be realistic and achievable. A COBRA is not constrained by the limitations of others. You cannot reach the stars without dreaming of them first. The greatest artists, inventors, creators, disruptors, scientists and general badasses were, are and always will be COBRAs.

Obstacles should be legitimate issues that could theoretically prevent you from reaching your goal. These may be people, places, temptations, distractions, fears etc. Think outside of the box. Make a list of anything that could attack your progress. The unknown can be terrifying. However if you are sincerely committed to reaching your goal, then you will find even more powerful optimal solutions to overcome any potential obstacles.

- **GOAL:** Visit the Sistine Chapel

- **ACTION:** Create an itinerary and budget.

- **OBSTACLE:** I don't have enough money.

- **OPTIMAL SOLUTION:** I save a few dollars a day.

Once you have finished the goal setting exercise I want you to find someone you trust and can confide in, this can be a spouse or trusted friend. Whoever that lucky devil is, hand them the thirty-day goals. Explain to them that in Exactly thirty days you would like to get together with them and open the envelope. You would like them to read your goals out loud and discuss how effective you were in achieving them.

→ BEGIN

Time to get into action. Time to take these goals and start making them a reality. Choose at least one action item from each category. Don't allow your self to get overwhelmed. Small but consistent action will yield huge results. Remember perfection almost never exists. The moment to undertake a new endeavor will never be ideal. If you always hesitate to attack until circumstances are perfect, you will miss many opportunities. Create opportunity through kinetic intention. Make a move in the direction of your goal and trust that the universe will reward forward momentum.

"A GOOD PLAN, VIOLENTLY EXECUTED NOW,
IS BETTER THAN A PERFECT PLAN NEXT WEEK"
-GENERAL GEORGE PATTON

→ REVIEW

Undertaking a new action frequently has unintended consequences and unexpected variables. The path to reach a goal rarely follows a straight line. Twists and turns are a part of the journey. The process requires that you remain self-aware, engage in self-diagnostics and make tweaks as you go along. Commit to reviewing your progress daily either before bed or in the morning. Anticipate any short term obstacles during the day that could derail you and adjust accordingly.

EXAMPLE #1 - I'm reading a book about basic finance.

- What's working? I've been disciplined each day dedicating time to reading.

- What isn't working? The material just isn't sticking. I feel like I'm wasting my time. It's so dry.

- Where are you making progress? I don't feel I am.
- Where do you feel stuck? I'm constantly distracted.

- What you can do differently to change any part of your action that isn't working? I can forget the book and try audio books or videos on YouTube. I can also listen to a finance audio-book while going on a thirty-minute walk which takes care of my physical commitment.

This is an excellent readjustment. Some people learn more effectively through listening or videos as opposed to reading. Combining physical activity with the revised auditory learning method may prove to be a vastly superior action plan than the initial one.

EXAMPLE #2 - I've joined a gym and started lifting weights.

- What's working? I enjoy the gym and it's social aspect.

- What isn't working? I'm beyond sore and my appetite has gone bonkers.
- Where do you feel you are making progress? I have noticed that I'm falling asleep more easily and sleeping more soundly.

- Where do you feel stuck? I feel like I need more information about proper technique for working out.

The phrase "working out" is beyond generic. If you are sore you need to review your pre-workout routine. Are you stretching? Are you staying properly hydrated to minimize the possibility of lactic acid buildup? Are you using proper technique when lifting weights?

Review your progress, weightlifting may not be the best source of exercise for you. You may benefit from yoga or a more cardio-based approach rather than resistance training. Consider asking for a personal trainer at the gym to take you through a work out and show you the proper techniques that are best suited for your body type and age and overall fitness goals.

Review your diet, increased appetite frequently occurs when you engage in resistance training. Have a low calorie, low sugar protein shake immediately after your workout. Here's a great out of the box tip: Television commercials about food are scientifically designed to trigger a hunger response. Reduce the amount of television you watch. Review these adjustments and keep fine tuning until you determine the best fit for you.

→ ADJUST

Attack your goals again utilizing the information and adjustments from the review of your progress. Continue to use the "begin, review, attack" loop as frequently as necessary. COBRAs remain flexible in their tactics depending upon changing circumstances and new information. Tactics are the specific actions taken to achieve a goal. If an action isn't working simply come up with a new action and try that one. Trial and error can be a very effective process when you eliminate and learn from what doesn't work. Creating a plan to achieve your goals demonstrates intelligence. Recognizing that life almost never accommodates plans demonstrates wisdom. Heavyweight boxing legend, Mike Tyson, hit the nail on the head when he said, "EVERYBODY HAS A PLAN UNTIL THEY GET PUNCHED IN THE MOUTH."

On rare occasions when desperate times call for extreme tactics you may consider what I call the NO PLAN B approach. The reversal to creating a contingency plan requires not having one. Sometimes if you want to take the island you must burn your boats like the conquistador, Hernan Cortez. He knew if he left his men with no option to retreat they would have to conquer or perish. Now that you have created your 30 day goals it's time to expand the horizon. Consider how the 30 day goals now serve as tactics in an overall strategy that will lead you to an overarching success in each area.

Before writing down new goals for the next year I want you to engage in two exercises. Do not censor or limit yourself. Have fun with this. Allow yourself to conjure up seemingly unrealistic possibilities. The first exercise I call... Aunt Tilly's Last Will and Testament.

> *Your beloved Aunt Tilly has passed on to the great beyond. You were always her favorite COBRA. You find yourself in the old country office of Jehoshaphat Wabash, Attorney at Law. Mr. Wabash informs you that as Aunt Tilly's only surviving heir, she has bequeathed you her entire estate of $30 million.*

I challenge you to ask yourself what you would do with such an extraordinary sum of money. How would this change your goals? Would you build your dream house? Travel the world? Quit your job and write the next great American novel? Or, would you become a philanthropist, helping as many people as possible? Make a list of some of the things you would like to do and accomplish.

Now for the second exercise. Yes, it will be every bit as extraordinary as the first one but very different. Brace yourself for...

A most unexpected visit to the doctor.

> *You receive a very short and somewhat cryptic message from the office of your doctor requesting that you please come to her office tomorrow morning at 9 AM. Remembering that you had taken a physical for your company's health insurance plan right after returning from your vacation, you figure this must be the results. The next day at Dr. Quigley's office she asks you to sit down. You oblige. She asks if you've been to the Tropics recently. You smile and reply, "Well yes, I was just on an island during my vacation several weeks ago." A look of gloom fills Dr. Quigley's face as she tells you that you've contracted a fatal and rare disease that only comes from the small island that you visited and that you have exactly one year to live.*

Armed with this information and unfortunately not Aunt Tilly's $30 million what goals do you seek to accomplish for your inevitable demise? Would you go on a skydiving tour of Europe? Would you spend your final year with friends and family? Would you finally get on stage and try stand up comedy? Make a list of all the goals you would pursue in your final year on the planet.

BROWN BELT

EXTERNAL

OBSTACLES

"You may not control all the events that happen to you, but you can decide not to be reduced by them."
                              -Maya Angelou

There are forces that exist among us that, either wittingly or unknowingly, separate you from your precious time, blow you off course or deplete your resources. Because society has trained you to be polite, accommodating and to a large extent compliant, you often hesitate to assert yourself against these external forces. In a nutshell, you don't like to be viewed as the bad guy, so you find yourself in the unenviable position of having your personal boundaries crossed by others. Ironically, you often feel guilty voicing your objections. Without a healthy set of boundaries or the ability to enforce them you find yourself the victim of external obstacles in the way of your success.

Typically external forces are considered beyond your control like political climate, the economy, natural disasters, and physical limitations, but COBRAs consider physical hindrances within our control as well. These include people, things and situations that drain your time, energy, resources and derail you from success. Many of your internal obstacles, if left unresolved, can become Emotional Vampires or Thieves of Time. It's important to identify your personal challenges and set a course to neutralize them. In doing so, you may attract or encounter new people into your biosphere. New-found confidence and success opens up the universe to attract all that you seek. It's important to be vigilant about who, what and even when you allow new people, things and experiences into your realm. Your brown belt will arm you with a basic set of tools necessary to recognize pitfalls and land mines, threats and imminent danger standing in the way of your black belt.

EMOTIONAL VAMPIRES

Emotional vampires assume many forms and often hardly look frightening at all. Frequently they are some of the people closest to you. That's what makes them so dangerous. They drain the life-force from your body robbing you of vital energy that should be directed towards productive endeavors. A classic version of the emotional vampire comes in the form of someone who constantly complains yet never looks for a solution. These types subconsciously feed off their own misery because it creates drama which gives them something to complain about. COBRAS DON'T COMPLAIN! We kick ass and problem solve. People who complain do it because it gives them an excuse to feel like a victim. VICTIMS DO NOT EXIST IN THIS DOJO! You must identify them and cut them out of your life or at least train them how to respect your time and boundaries.

WE TRAIN PEOPLE HOW TO TREAT US.
-MICHELE KANAN

Emotional Vampires are especially dangerous when they are young ... well, your youngsters. My wife and I have five children so I know of what I speak, oh yes, your Sensei married a woman with four teenagers. I was a single guy and a very part-time dad until we moved in together and I became an instant full-time dad to five children... four girls and one boy. The saving grace was that my wife had a black belt in mothering and was not afraid to use it. She gave me the crash course which includes pearls like

- Kids are born tiny sociopaths, it's our job to parent them into good citizens.

- The more attention you give them the more they want, so make sure that you instill a sense of appreciation for your time in them by teaching them unconditional love.

- The inmates outnumber the guards, so do not allow any dissension in the ranks or breaks in the chain of command.

As with any new romance, we wanted time to be a couple, instead we were a couple with an audience. It was very easy to fall into the emotional traps associated with blending families but setting boundaries and clear communication saved us from becoming another statistic. The magic trick of how we did it is a story for another time, and hers to tell.

Family

Family is full of emotional vampires because there is so much history of supporting each other and duty. Your only defense is to set clear boundaries and make the most of your time together. Theres is no shame in redirecting the conversation with a family member that lives to dump their problems and complaints on you. It's self-preservation to say "I know you've suffered a lot, but it would mean a lot to me if you could tell me about something positive in your life so I don't worry about you." By using clear language with an attainable and positive message, you effectively put the negative emotional spew on pause, clearing the way for a happy exchange.

Lesser Companions

Lesser companions start off feeding your ego because you are so much better, smarter, prettier, skinnier, more talented, richer or whatever they perceive you are better at in a time when your self-esteem is at a low point. They seem to crave your knowledge, experience and humility. That is until the emotional boomerang circles back with their demands on your time to reassure them that they are worthy of you and your time. Resist the temptation, if you can't, watch Fatal Attraction with Glenn Close. Every time you see a bunny, it will remind you to be a COBRA.

Work

Work is stressful even if you are lucky enough to be doing what you love. That stress can suck the emotion out of you, sending you home an empty, exhausted shell. Set boundaries to separate your professional life from your personal life. It's ok to go above and beyond from time to time, but making yourself perpetually available may earn you a couple extra bucks, but you spend it on repairing your mental health.

World Events

The world and social landscape are full of landmines, traps and deception. Information flows faster than the speed of thought.

Your emotions are flooded non-stop with one scary story and a terrifying one after a traumatic one. Stop the madness. We have world leaders to deal with the issues in our absence making it okay to unplug on a regular basis without becoming a bad citizen.

▦ Money

Financial woes can be emotionally draining whether it's not having enough now or planning for the future. Although money needs vigilant protection, you need a break. Discipline yourself to shut down your money woes after 10pm. Nothing can happen in the financial system until 9am, so there's no use worrying about it every night. Excessive worry never fixed anything except sleepiness.

"IF IT CAN BE SOLVED. THERE'S NO NEED
TO WORRY. AND IF IT CAN'T BE SOLVED.
WORRY IS OF NO USE."
- DALAI LAMA.

THIEVES OF TIME

The emotional vampire's partner in crime is the Thief of Time. Their larceny may prove even more destructive as they rob you of your finite and most valuable resource, time. While Thieves of Time often appear in the form of a person, make no mistake that they are not limited solely to animated beings. They come in the form of excessive time wasted on television or video games. The worst thieves of time rear their ugly heads in the shape of our vices. Imagine how much time you waste if you are a smoker. Break it down mathematically. If the average smoke takes even a minute and you smoke a pack a day that's twenty minutes spent being a slave to something that is killing you. Multiply that by 365 days and you have wasted more than five entire days. Imagine what you could accomplish in that time.

As I finally sit down to write this today I feel a bit harried and rushed. I wanted to be writing several hours earlier but couldn't seem to find the time. How often have we all glommed on to that familiar story? Sometimes even Sensei finds himself competing for time at the hands of others. Now, clearly it's my responsibility to martial my time in an effective way. Make no mistake about it. "I couldn't find the time" is an excuse, nothing but a story you perpetuate as a means to rationalize procrastination or failure to meet time sensitive objectives. I have come to learn after years of battling, it's an art or at least a learned skill set. When something is truly important you make time to do it. Just think about the last time you were in the early stages of falling in love. You moved heaven and earth to see the object of your desire.

LIKE SANDS THROUGH THE HOURGLASS SO ARE THE DAYS OF OUR LIVES.

Possibly the most profound words ever uttered from the world of Daytime television. Apart from your physical well being, time is the most precious commodity in the universe. It can neither be bought nor sold. It cannot be stopped nor can it be returned once taken. This is why you must constantly be vigilant towards those who seek to deprive you of it either intentionally or unconsciously. This is your precious life, my friend. There's no dress rehearsal.

COBRA SENSITIVITY

While a COBRA should be attuned to the emotions of others and sensitive to their feelings, that's not the type of sensitivity I'm talking about. I'm referring to sensitivity and awareness to your surroundings. People, places and things. Situational awareness, a mindset that can save your life. Both a cobra and a COBRA possess excellent situational awareness. They are aware of any possible threat in their immediate environment and constantly calculate how to minimize and deal with any potential danger. Cobras in the wild possess highly developed senses including a keen sense of smell and well adapted night vision. They act instinctively, recognizing danger immediately thereby allowing them to avoid it or preemptively attack. You must learn to refine your abilities to read people whether in a bar, on the street or in the office. As we learn about ourselves, we become better equipped to overcome our internal obstacles. As we learn about others and the world around us, we become better attuned to handle external obstacles.

The secret of situational awareness is to anticipate a threat before it materializes rather than react once faced with it. Human beings have honed their instincts for eons, trust yours. Use your senses and watch for red flags. The United States military utilizes a readiness and alert system known as DEF-CON which is short for defense condition.

There are four stages ranging from DEF-CON one to DEF-CON four. Think of it like this. DEF-CON one you're having a burger with friends but always aware of your surroundings and tracking the general activity you see. DEF-CON four is go time. In our dojo we use a simpler system based on three colors, yellow, red and green. These three colors each indicate a different level of readiness in dealing with any potential threat.

☞ GREEN - Should always be your baseline. It's a relaxed state of readiness however you remain engaged and aware.

Generally this applies to a situation that's a known entity of relative safety. You may be at home or a place you know well that has a very low likelihood of threat. You have scanned the surroundings and made a mental check of people, places and things deeming the current situation very low threat. If you are home this means you have checked the locks, know exactly who

142

is in your home and have a clear idea where your emergency equipment and home protection weapons are situated.

> ⊡ YELLOW - Heightened level of awareness. All of your senses should be focused on gathering as much information as possible. Mentally review plans for fight or flight. It can be triggered at any time from the potential of a perceived threat.

This may come in the form of an individual behaving strangely due to mental illness, intoxication or loud and menacing behavior or a dangerous or unknown environment. Remember the Terminator? His neuroprocessor generates a rapid amount of incoming information detailing everything in the vicinity. This information determined various courses of action to neutralize or avoid any threats. The condition YELLOW means you are eliminating distractions, determining options and preparing for the possibility of potential kinetic action.

> † RED - A threat is verified and imminent. You are now fully focused and ready to act.

Anytime you use physical violence against another individual it MUST be a last resort. You also need to be very clear that once physical violence is used for anything beyond self-defense it's not only morally wrong but you are opening yourself up to criminal prosecution and civil lawsuit. Defend yourself when necessary but tread lightly. Always attempt to deescalate first. Many times physical conflict can be avoided with simple good manners, civility and an occasional apology. It's far better to swallow your pride sometimes than your teeth. If possible always attempt to walk away.

Situational awareness differs depending on people, places and things. Each of these presents the possibility of different threats and requires different responses. Here are some strategies that you can use to identify and minimize threats.

PEOPLE

"BE POLITE. BE PROFESSIONAL. BUT HAVE A PLAN TO KILL EVERYBODY YOU MEET."

-GENERAL JAMES "MAD DOG" MATTIS

General Mattis is a great leader and a true hero. But, he was most likely speaking as a soldier. You aren't soldiers and fortunately not at war so with all due respect to the general for the purposes of our dojo we will turn the volume down just a bit. Let's go with "be polite, be professional, but have a plan to defend yourself if necessary with everyone you meet."

Human beings far and away present the largest potential threat. There are seven billion of us, all with distinct and different personalities. That makes us unpredictable. Lack of predictability is a definite variable in threat. Now look, most people consider themselves to be good and decent. A fairly high percentage of them are. A COBRA does not go through life paranoid, suspicious and living in fear. However trust must be earned and unfortunately there are some bad "machines" out there with some very screwed up wiring. A COBRA understands human psychology and can quickly identify individuals with dangerous psychological qualities. I consulted with Dr. Robi Ludwig, a practicing NYC psychotherapist and celebrated author, to gain some more insight into these human land mines. Human beings constantly attempt to hide their true emotions, intentions and agenda. Focus less on what people say and more on what they do and how they act. You must familiarize yourself with behavior patterns and personality traits of this next group of individuals.

They present danger to COBRAs ranging from mildly destructive to potentially catastrophic. Many people possess a few characteristics found in the descriptions below. This does not mean that your grandmother who at times seems superficially charming and occasionally tells whoppers qualifies as a psychopath. There is a clear difference between difficult people and individuals with legitimate narcissistic personality disorder and anti social personality disorder.

NARCISSISTS

The moniker Narcissist has become a pop-culture reference to any individual overly concerned with themselves. Do not confuse narcissists with individuals who have Narcissistic Personality Disorder (NPD). There is a difference. People with NPD are a subset found in the psychiatric diagnosis of Antisocial Personality Disorder, a true mental illness. While not all of them are dangerous they can be. NPD is a frequent characteristic found in serial killers. These characters are not merely overcompensating for feelings of inadequacy and low self esteem, they legit see themselves as all that and a bag of chips. COBRA or not, you won't be able to alter that perception. So do not waste your time. Narcissists as opposed to individuals with NPD are not generally violent or overly destructive. They do however become tedious, irritating and generally suck the oxygen out of every room. Left unchecked they will undoubtedly become emotional vampires monopolizing your time with their insanity.

The spectrum for NPD is wide, ranging from individuals with an overly elevated sense of self-confidence to textbook self-grandiosity. While the individual with an overdeveloped sense of self-confidence may seem overbearing, obnoxious and in some ways socially awkward, those folks suffering from clinical narcissistic grandiosity are relatively easy to recognize. Their sense of self borders on the unbelievable. If you find yourself trying to suppress the urge to roll your eyes every time you hear one of their self important stories, take note.

The potential pitfall with narcissists is that they initially can make a great first impression appearing charismatic and seductive. They are frequently physically attractive. Because they put so much attention on how others perceive them they tend to be highly concerned with their physical appearance and are frequently appealing at first glance. They view their sexuality and external appearance as a formidable weapon to manipulate others.

IDENTIFYING CHARACTERISTICS

Narcissists paint themselves as the hero or victim in **every** one of their stories depending on what best serves them in the moment. Look for this recurring theme. Narcissists consistently position themselves as the center of attention because their sense of self requires constant attention from others. They frequently over exaggerate their credits in the arenas of business, education, and interaction regarding sexual relationships and romantic attachments. They expect others to view them as superior even though they do not possess the credentials to support this. They exhibit thoughtlessness in the face of unrealistic expectations for others to cater to their whims.

Narcissists often struggle with some form of addiction in an attempt to re-create feelings of euphoria when they feel on top of the world. When the feeling dissipates they must re-engage in the behavior reinforcing the cycle of addiction. Drugs and alcohol, at least in the short term, are an instant and reliable way to restore their feeling of omnipotence.

Social media is a handy tool to identify these Emotional Vampires. They are often excessively involved with taking "selfies", social media posting and the obsessive pursuit of likes and followers. Through social media they can present themselves in a completely controlled and very positive light. Additionally they are not required to show their "friends" the normal considerations for actual in person authentic relationships.

DEALING WITH NARCISSISTS

The best solution is very simple...DON'T. They usually out themselves within a relatively short amount of time, they can't hold in all the glory that is them. Once the gig is up as to who they really are, others begin to cut off their lifeblood: attention. They also shake out as highly untrustworthy. If you're lucky they will self-implode.

If you find yourself in a workplace environment with one of these special snowflakes you may have to put on your dancing shoes, (as in tap dancing around their need for attention and flattery), or do your best to stay off their radar. Be very careful not to become entangled romantically with a narcissist. It will generate frustration, anger, and possibly heartbreak. If you become the object of their affection and you don't reciprocate, look out. Narcissists do not take well to rejection and disappointment. They may likely respond with highly manipulative, passive aggressive behavior or actively attempt to malign or sabotage you.

SOCIOPATHS

Antisocial Personality Disorder (APD) is a diagnosis resulted from learned behavior and or trauma, referred to as Sociopaths. They are not born but developed. It's estimated that sociopaths make up between 3% and 5% of the population. Sociopathy is more prevalent within the male population but well represented with females. So, it's a pretty good bet that you've already encountered several and if by some miracle you haven't, trust me, you will. Sociopaths can present as very charming however, this act masks their true personality which is generally highly deceptive, prone to erratic behavior, risk-taking, lying, elevated anger tendencies coupled with a general lack of empathy. These individuals possess a disturbing capability of mimicking socially acceptable "nice" behavior when it serves their needs. They almost always know right from wrong but don't let that stand in their way when it comes to getting what they want.

Although sociopaths have the capacity to participate in relationships they are generally fraught with one type of chaos or another. A sociopath involved in a romantic relationship doesn't experience a deep and profound connection the way the rest of us do when we are in love. They view their partner as a prize rather than an equal. The relationship almost always suffers due to its relative superficiality in the mind of the sociopath.

IDENTIFYING CHARACTERISTICS

Often intelligent, charismatic and superficially charming, Sociopaths employ excessive praise and compliments as a strategy to ingratiate themselves and manipulate others, or I like to call a "love bomb". A COBRA derives his or her sense of worth from within, but appreciates compliments when they're genuine and appropriate. If someone's praise and compliments feel ill-timed or disproportionate, be wary.

Sociopaths have difficulty maintaining employment. They believe that the rules do not apply to them and they have little respect for authority. Sociopaths will tend to keep to themselves in the workplace interacting with others only when it serves them. They are often quick to claim undeserved credit and assign unmerited blame to others when things go South. To make matters worse they seem to take a perverse pleasure in watching others receiving punishment.

Sociopaths are often uncomfortably and overly familiar with strangers or restaurant staff and therefore, frequently lie and spread calculated gossip. Remember character is the first pillar of WOTC. Character is everything. If someone lies to you once it may simply be confused communication. It happens. A second lie represents a gross mistake that should register a big red flag. A third lie should display a flashing exit sign and tells you it's time to get the hell out of Dodge. Clearly you're dealing with an untrustworthy individual. Additionally, Sociopaths never apologize or admit fault. If they do it is not out of genuine remorse but rather for effect. A COBRA's friendship is a very special thing and not to be granted to someone who has a significant problem with truthfulness.

Sociopaths, depending where they are on the sliding scale, can present legitimate danger. Their brain chemistry does not function like normal people which has the net effect of making them deceitful and unconcerned with others people and their property. They often engage in reckless behavior, risk-taking and fail to conform to society's norms.

Do your best not to engage with someone you suspect to be a sociopath. If it is unavoidable be clear with yourself about who they are. Do not expect them to play by the rules or demonstrate a sense of fairness. They may occasionally mention suicide largely for calculated emotional effect rather than a legitimate threat. Divulge nothing or as little personal information as possible, but take care not to offend them by attempting to verify their stories. Sociopaths often look for "marks" to target, so don't be an easy one. Be alert to someone asking you probing questions about yourself yet subtly avoiding sharing about themselves. Sociopaths are excellent emotional detectives. They will attempt to learn all about you then match their personality to whom they think you want them to be. They do this to prod for points of weakness. Project strength but do not antagonize them. Never forget they may easily resort to physical violence or hostile action against you. Always be on moderate alert when in close proximity.

PSYCHOPATHS

Sociopaths and psychopaths are frequently confused but there are some highly significant differences. All psychopaths are sociopaths but not all sociopaths are psychopaths. These nightmarish unicorns are born not made. Psychopaths, through no fault of their own, left the womb with no conscience. If that isn't bad enough, they have a greatly diminished sense of fear and are less affected by distress due to their dramatically different brain chemistry and hardwiring. Psychopaths differ from sociopaths in that they tend to not want to call attention to themselves and have the ability to plot and act with less impulsiveness and greater calculation.

Some psychopaths are able to achieve significant success running corporations, becoming surgeons, lawyers and even police officers. It is not inconceivable that you will encounter one of these individuals if you haven't already. This ability to blend in allows them to fly under the radar creating a perfect storm for criminal behavior. It is estimated that psychopaths are approximately twenty times more likely to engage in criminal behavior. This doesn't mean that psychopathy always produces arch criminal, Hannibal "the Cannibal" Lecter but they certainly have the potential if exposed to that environment.

IDENTIFYING CHARACTERISTICS

Superficially charming and glib, surprisingly many functioning psychopaths are well liked. They are quite often engaging and gifted storytellers drawing on their grandiosity and arrogance as pathological liars. Psychopaths are highly manipulative demonstrating a complete lack of empathy. They do not experience real feelings of remorse or guilt because they have no conscience. Instead, they "read the room" and deliver the text book response necessary to advance their agenda. If they are ever abruptly made aware that they may have insulted or hurt someone they may respond by saying "so and so should lighten up" or "they are too sensitive" or worse yet "they had it coming".

Psychopaths tend to have a lower resting heart rate. This means they're cool cucumbers when things get chaotic. Crying for psychopaths is very problematic. When "normal" individuals cry actual emotionally based tears, they cry with two eyes wiping both eyes at the same time. Psychopaths frequently wipe the bottom of each eye individually because they are primarily affecting sadness rather than feeling it.

Psychopaths speak slightly differently than the rest of us. They utilize verbs in the past tense with greater frequency. By speaking in the past tense it is believed they are distancing themselves from their actions. We might say "I believe it's the best option" while Mr. Psychopath might say "I believed it was the best option". This assertion that he acted in what he believed was the best possible way intends to mitigate any damaging behavior and deflect responsibility and ownership. Psychopaths tend to use more words like "um" and "err" to create conversational pauses in an attempt to appear more normal.

DEALING WITH PSYCHOPATHS

Avoid these individuals if at all possible. Trust your instincts. Humans often have an uneasy physical reaction to people perceived as predators, it seems we are hardwired that way. Psychopaths also seem to be hardwired to determine which individuals present an increased probability they can be victimized. Do not show weakness and vulnerability. These individuals thrive on that. This is bad. Remain calm. Convey a sense of strength and the ability to defend yourself but do not become overly aggressive. Remain measured and seek to deescalate conflict. If that isn't possible and escape isn't an alternative you fight like hell. Remember you are a COBRA.

If interacting with a psychopath in a business situation remember that they thrive on dominance. If you can provide them with a win-win scenario explaining logically that they would be better working with you than against you, they may take it. If you find yourself in a negotiation situation with a psychopath do your best to conduct correspondence by email. Make negotiations as clinical and impersonal as possible. Psychopaths tend to do much better face-to-face where they can intimidate, manipulate, and generally play head games. Using a relatively impersonal form of communication like email limits their bag of tricks.

GASLIGHTING

The term originated from a play in the 1930s in which a sociopathic husband undermines his wife's sense of sanity by causing her to question what she is experiencing. In reality he had been orchestrating a series of confusing events in an attempt to institutionalize her for financial gain. "Gaslighting" became a part of the national lexicon after the play was adapted into a film starring Charles Boyer, Joseph Cotten and Ingrid Bergman.

Gaslighting is a nefarious and pernicious tactic of manipulation, Malignant narcissists, destructive sociopaths and dangerous psychopaths utilize it to gain psychological power and control over their target. They achieve this by feeding erroneous information to the victim with the goal of causing the victim to question their recall, perception of events in conversations, and ultimately their sense of sanity and reality.

TACTICS

The perpetrator establishes trust and intimacy through compliments and flattery posing as a loving and concerned friend. The gaslighter continues to build trust with the victim like by sharing something "personal". Then, the gaslighter begins making disparaging comments, *ad hominem* jokes, directs "concerned" criticism testing the victims boundaries. The gaslighter will tell the victim and anyone else they can snare in their web of deceit that the victim is "too sensitive", "needs to lighten up", "doesn't understand humor", etc... all of these dismissive phrases are meant to distance the gaslighter from their abusive behavior while eroding the victim's credibility in the eyes of others and in the victim's own eyes. The gaslighter begins telling small lies initiating confusion and doubt in the victim.

At this point two things begin to happen. The victim initially doesn't want to believe that their friend or loved one would systematically manipulate and injure them. The gaslighter vehemently denies their actions or words even when confronted with incontrovertible evidence to the contrary. The gaslighter further creates a sense of uncertainty by periodically employing positive reinforcement to the victim creating a cycle of doubt and confusion. The intended result is to cause the victim to question their own judgment. The gaslighter will attempt to turn family, friends and coworkers against the victim once the victim begins to question the gaslighter's behavior. At this point the gaslighter will try to get everyone to view the victim as paranoid and delusional and eventually questioning their sanity. The gaslighter will seek to erode the victim's support system and place the victim in a position where they have to defend their sense of reality to themselves and those around them. Gaslighting reaches its maximum effect when the target questions their own memory, recall and sanity.

How does a COBRA defend against gaslighting?

Don't take it personally. Gaslighters have significant self-esteem issues. They have an innate need to feel superior just to feel equal to others. Identify the pattern of psychologically manipulative conduct employed by the gaslighter. The inability of the victim to recognize what is happening makes the gaslighting effective and obscures the gaslighter's true intentions. Once you notice that you're the victim of gaslighting begin to keep a journal writing down dates, times, lies and inconsistencies. Know that most likely you will not be able to change the gaslighter's behavior through emotional appeals, logic or rationalization.

Sever or minimize the relationship slowly. Spend time with supportive friends and family. Consider seeking therapy to process the damage that was done. If you were in a romantic relationship with an individual who has been gaslighting you, some major soul-searching is in your future. If they are willing to undergo couples therapy that may remedy the issue however if they resist then it's time to pull the ripcord and end the relationship.

If your family member is the gaslighter distance yourself and consider calling a family meeting or intervention to confront the individual. Make certain to have evidence from your journal to make your case. Don't go into the process with the goal of humiliating or destroying the gaslighter. Try to use the opportunity to unify and heal the family while getting the gaslighter to accept responsibility or at least understand that their behavior will not be tolerated.

If you have been the subject of gaslighting from your boss or co-worker, the only viable solution is to leave your place of employment. It may seem extreme, but desperate times call for desperate measures and COBRAs act decisively. It may sting in the beginning, but in the long run you will be better off starting over with a clean slate before things get out of hand. Try to obtain a positive recommendation if possible, but no job is worth your sanity and self-esteem.

BEWARE OF THE MONGOOSE

Remember COBRA's are not paranoid and definitely try to see the good in all people. However a COBRA realizes that not all people behave with integrity or positive intentions, they are called mongoose in this dojo. The mongoose is the natural enemy of the cobra, just as ill-meaning menaces are the natural enemy of COBRAs. You must know how to identify these people, and defend yourself from them.

The ability to recognize potentially threatening body language is an invaluable tool. Identifying potential threats based on someone's overt behavior is generally pretty easy. We've all felt the hair on the back of our neck stand up when we come in contact with someone whose behavior is obviously "off". It can range from the drunk and obstreperous guy at the bar to the maniac in the car next to you wearing a tee shirt that reads "Road rage. Not just for breakfast anymore." Spotting these individuals is pretty darn easy.

Reading the more subtle body language that can proceed a threat takes a little more work but it's well worth your time and can save your life. The ability to read body language warns us of imminent threats and the emotional mindset of an individual. Here are some physical tells that could mean trouble.

- WEAPONS-first and foremost scan for any potential weapons. Look for a knife hooked inside a front pocket. Look for a bulge through the ankles possibly indicating a gun. If an individual is wearing a jacket, especially a heavy leather jacket, they can easily be concealing a multitude of weapons. Assume they have one and if they do they will use it.

- ENCROACHING ON PERSONAL SPACE - when someone gets too close to you, physically, there should be a red flag. In a self-defense situation you always want to maintain distance so that you have the ability to react. It is nearly impossible to block a punch or a headbutt from a few inches away. Be aware that an individual may not always initially appear threatening when confronting you. Sometimes they may do the exact opposite as a false flag. They may try to appear friendly.

- CLENCHING - be aware if somebody's jaw is clenching or their hand is balled up into a fist.

153

HEAD POSITION - Watch for head movement when an individual is directly in front of you. If their head dips and begins to turn away this is a pretty good indication they're about to throw a punch. Go with your gut and use your instincts. Strike first with overwhelming violence. Generally in a fight whoever gets the first punch off has a greater chance of winning.

POINTING - If someone is standing in front of you aggressively pointing at you or poking your chest, this is an immediate indication that you need to go to condition RED. If you observe someone pointing at you from a distance in a bar or on the street and you don't know this individual immediately go to condition YELLOW.

BODY POSITION - if someone is standing before you visibly upset but their arms are crossed, make certain that you've created some space and go to condition YELLOW. If they are "blading" their body which means they have turned to an angle minimizing themselves as a target, this is an excellent indication that they may be getting ready to attack. Bring both of your hands up to chest level with your left hand resting on top of your right hand (if you're a lefty it would be right on top of left.) This is a non-threatening position but will allow you to quickly attack or defend. If you were faced with multiple threatening individuals never let anyone get behind you. Also avoid having your back against the wall. At this point you have three choices: Deescalate, leave if possible or fight. If you are faced with a necessity to fight, focus on one individual. Attack first and attack viciously. Your inclination may be to attack as many as you can one after the other. Overwhelm one individual and you have a reasonable chance that the others won't want to engage. If that's not the case then know that most likely you are going to be punched, you are going to be hurt but you must fight for your life. Especially in our current climate you cannot count upon help from the police.

FACIAL EXPRESSIONS - It doesn't take a brain surgeon to infer when someone's face indicates they're pissed off. Look at the eyes. Dilated pupils indicate an influx of adrenaline and that the "fight or flight" systems in the body have been triggered. Blood pressure generally increases when an individual is getting ready to attack. Often you can see their face become flushed and red and the veins in their neck and head become more prominent. Condition RED.

PLACES

Many environments can pose a threat. A COBRA is always aware of their surroundings.

▣ HOME - with few exceptions your home should be the safest place in the world. Generally speaking you can remain at condition GREEN. That is assuming that you take a few steps.

▣ Make certain that your doors and windows are locked.

▣ Know where your keys are in the event that you have to exit the house quickly. The same goes for your wallet or purse.

▣ Know where any weapons are at all times. Make certain that they are easily accessible if needed. It goes without saying that they are in proper working order. If you're not comfortable with a firearm then I suggest you get a can of bear mace, a baseball bat or at least a nice set of steak knives.

▣ You should also have a bug-out bag. In the event that you have to jam. It should contain cash, prepaid credit cards, food and water for several days, a weapon, rope, electrical tape, any critical medication and a small transistor radio for starters.

▣ For added security you can turn your alarm on the perimeter so that you will be alerted immediately if any doors are opened.

VEHICLE

We spent a great deal of time in our cars and as such they are frequently the site of dangerous threats.

▣ Maintain some kind of weapon in your car. Make sure that you know how to effectively use it.

▣ I also suggest having a sharp knife in the event that you need to cut your seatbelt. Look for a knife that has a knob on the handle that can be used for breaking a window.

▣ You will also want to have an emergency bag much like your bug-out bag in the trunk. Include jumper cables, tire repair kit, flashlight, flares, a lighter, some basic toiletries, critical medication, a rain poncho and a small, empty, plastic gas container as well as some basic first aid items, water and protein bars.

- Never leave valuables in your car or mail with your home address. In reality, using a PO Box is the best decision. Do not register your home address as "home" in your navigation system.

TAXIS

- Always look at the driver's photo and driver ID number.

- Take note of the taxi's identification number which is found on the outside of the cab.

- Take note of the driver's name on the Hack license which is generally on the passenger side of the dashboard. If the driver's name is something common, mention in passing that your brother or sister has the same name. This is a subtle way to let them know you are aware and will remember their name.

BUSES, TRAINS AND SUBWAYS -

- All public transportation are just that, public. That means that any wide variety of characters will be your fellow travelers.

- Sit near the front on buses in view of the driver and CCTV camera.

- Remain aware of each stop and where you are getting off.

- Scan each passenger when getting on the bus.

- Observe everyone who gets on and off the bus.

- When exiting the bus observe anyone who gets off after you to make sure you aren't being followed.

- Be wary of anyone striking up a conversation and asking questions about your stop, transportation habits, employment etc. There is a difference between being civil and being naive.

- Pay attention to your intuition.

PLANES

Much of this advice also applies to the previous methods of

transportation. I conferred with a friend of mine who is a federal Air Marshal and she helped me with the following advice.

- Do not make the mistake of placing your travel plans on social media platforms. Confirm with all family members that they understand. This obviously applies for any trip.

- While it isn't always possible you should try to avoid checking your bags. Make certain to have a unique colored ribbon or ID tag attached to your luggage. Do not put your full name and home address on the ID tag, instead put an email address. The goal is to make your bags easily identifiable to you while not attracting unwanted attention.

- Once on the plane before taking your seat locate and make a mental note of your nearest emergency exit. Frequently these emergency exit doors will be behind you rather than in front of you.

- The specter of a hijacking is not a pleasant thought. Each seating position has pros and cons. Aisle seats provide easier access allowing you to get up and move quickly during an emergency. Conversely they render you more exposed to attack from the aisle way. A window seat creates a buffer and distance between you and any potential attack. It also places the individual in the aisle seat in the position of acting as a shield. Consider this carefully. This may sound cold but there's a difference between a family member and a stranger.
- A beverage cart in the aisle presents a formidable obstacle in your mobility. Generally these carts are secured with brakes on the wheels considering the fact that they weigh several hundred pounds.

- Observe the other passengers. Initiate this while at the gate area before boarding. Look for anyone who is behaving oddly. Any abnormal behavior such as intoxication or excessive nervousness should be noted. You will want to keep an eye on these individuals. Remember, if you see something say something.

- In the event that you must defend yourself, you must think outside the box. Airplane security is specifically geared to prevent passengers from bringing anything that can function as a weapon on the plane. That however does not mean there are not weapons at your disposal. A tightly rolled magazine makes a formidable weapon when jammed into someone's exposed throat. The hard edge of a laptop, tablet or hardcover book also works in a pinch as does throwing scalding coffee in someone's face. Thinking defensively, use a rolled up jacket or blanket around your arm to defend against knives.

OFFICE BUILDINGS

▦ Familiarize yourself with the location of exits, stairwells and elevators.

▦ Be observant of any odd behavior from coworkers or unfamiliar faces.

▦ Have a plan in the event of an active shooter situation. Know how to get out, hide or fight.

▦ Have a bug-out backpack. This may sound extreme however if you work in a major metropolitan city that could suffer and attack, black out or any other unforeseen calamity, you'll be happy you have it. You may have to walk for long distances through chaotic and unsafe areas. Think immediate survival. A weapon, cash, map of the city, food and water. This should not take up a lot of space and can be left in a drawer at your desk. Critical infrastructure and communication grids could be down. Do not count on your cellphone working.

HOTELS

▦ Check-in - Request the front desk employee writes your room number rather than announce it out loud. You never know who may be listening. It can be another guest or a staff member.

▦ Avoid giving your room number out unless necessary.

▦ Avoid the ground floor. They provide the easiest access for unwanted entrance by an intruder. Conversely avoid the very top floors in the event of a fire.

▦ When entering your room check it out thoroughly including the closets and under the bed.

▦ Confirm that the locks in the room are in working order. If there is a safe confirm that it also works.

- Always bring a flashlight when you travel to a hotel. In the event of a fire if the hallways are full of smoke you'll be very happy to have it.

- Always have some form of protection in the room. This can be pepper spray, a knife or whatever you feel most comfortable.

- If you are alone in a hotel room keep the door open when someone enters. Never make yourself vulnerable to an erroneous complaint of inappropriate behavior.

- If you find anyone in your room not specifically invited by you, including hotel staff, leave the room and report it immediately. Do not wait to hear an explanation.

- If you lose or misplace your room key, report it immediately to the front desk. If possible request a room change. Your key may have been unknowingly stolen from you by an individual with bad intentions.

- When parking, spend the extra couple bucks and valet the car. Make sure that there are no valuables in the car or information identifying who you are or where you live. If valet is not an option, park as close to the elevator and exit in the parking structure as possible. Be aware that if you were parked close to a stairwell with easy access to an exit, it also provides an excellent hiding place for anyone posing a threat. Be vigilant when walking especially if you are alone.

- Hotel bars can be lots of fun. They can also be a magnet for potential threats because of their transient nature, it's difficult to notice when someone doesn't belong. When people are drinking, inhibitions are greatly reduced and the large majority of people are most likely strangers. Be aware. Never accept a drink from someone you do not know. Never leave your drink then come back to it and drink it.

ON THE STREET

- Do not look like a victim. Walk with confidence and purpose.

- Stop occasionally and subtly take a 360 degree assessment of your surroundings.

- Do not make protracted eye contact with anyone as it can be inferred as an act of aggression.

159

- Talking mindlessly on your phone is like ringing the dinner bell for predators. They can see that you are distracted making you an excellent target.

- Be vigilant of anyone following you for a protracted period of time.

- If you're under the influence of excessive alcohol, it is better to take a taxi or use a rideshare app than just stumble around on the street. This is another dinner bell. Call a friend from the car to put any creeper in the driver's seat on notice that someone is imminently expecting you. Also, share your route with the same friend. If a hotel/motel is nearby, get a room and sleep it off. The money you spend on the room is a lot cheaper than a funeral.

Remember the key to situational awareness is to anticipate the danger and avoid it before it ever happens brilliantly illustrated by this story about a Samurai and his sons. Samurais are known for their situational awareness.

THE   SAMURAI   AND   HIS   THREE   SONS

*M*any *years ago in feudal Japan, in a small and unremarkable province, there lived an old samurai. And although he came from a small and unremarkable province he was renowned throughout the land as a swordsman beyond compare plus a wise and gifted Sensei. His beloved wife Kumiko had long since passed away and he lived with his three sons; each of them at different stages in their training to become samurai. Coming to the realization that he was rapidly approaching the end of his years, he needed to make the decision which of his three sons would succeed him at his dojo.*

As a test, he summoned them, asking them to wait outside the door of their home. Inside he positioned a small pillow above the door so that when the door was opened the pillow would fall to the ground. The first son, the youngest of the three, impetuously walked through the front door and a pillow promptly fell upon his head. He bowed his head in disgrace and returned outside. The old samurai returned inside the home to reposition the pillow. The second son drew three deep breaths, focused his attention and opened the door. He had taken but one step into the home when the pillow began to fall. With almost unimaginable lightning speed he drew his katana expertly cutting the pillow in two. Again the old samurai returned inside the home and yet again repositioned one half of the pillow. The oldest son approached the door, closed his eyes for an instant as an almost in perceivable smile flashed across his face. He turned around and walked back to his two brothers.

The old samurai now stood in front of his three sons. He looked upon his oldest son with just the slightest hint of pride and then bowed to him. Saying "It is my oldest son who truly embodies the essence of samurai. While your skill with the Katana is undeniable, it is your ability to sense danger and avoid it which is truly remarkable. It is you who shall be called Sensei.

BLACK BELT

A TALE

OF TWO

COBRAS

"I must also have a dark side
if I am to be whole."
-Carl Jung

Within all of us lives a dark side. Competition between our positive and negative sides churns like a flowing river, sometimes quietly, and occasionally with rage and fury. We require the best parts of both forces to be complete.

I must now digress. I'm an old-school, unrepentant Trekkie.

Stardate 2772.1. Director Leo Penn, father of another famous Penn, helmed Star Trek episode five of the first season, "The Enemy Within." After beaming down to the very inhospitable planet, Alpha 177, Captain James Tiberius Kirk finds himself on the receiving end of a very serious transporter malfunction separating him into two identical Captain Kirks. One represents his "good" side, kind, just and compassionate. The other, highly aggressive, violent and emotionally irrational. The "good" Kirk soon becomes aware that his doppelganger is running a muck causing havoc throughout the Enterprise. The conflict centers around Kirk's rapidly declining ability to exercise the power of command. He begins demonstrating marked weakness specifically in situations requiring decisiveness and leadership. Mr. Spock reluctantly points out that if Captain Kirk continues to diminish in capacity he will have to relinquish command. Furthermore Spock hypothesizes that the "good" Kirk needs the "evil" one to effectively command not only the ship but himself. Although repugnant and destructive, the "evil" Kirk possesses the strength, force of will and aggressiveness required to command others and a Federation starship. Ultimately the "good" Kirk carries the physically diminished "evil" Kirk into the now properly functioning transporter. Spock dematerializes both Kirks. Captain Kirk reemerges as his normal and reintegrated, heroic self.

I would like to share a well-worn parable to further illustrate the concept of duality and the importance of balancing both. It's passed down verbally from generation to generation, it remains unknown exactly where and with whom it originated, but it illustrates a universal truth.

A wise snake-charmer seeks to teach his grandson about life:"A fight rages inside me," he said to the boy. "It is a terrible fight between two cobras. One is made of darkness; he burns with anger, envy, sorrow, regret, greed, arrogance, self-pity, guilt, resentment, inferiority, lies, false pride, superiority and ego." The wise, snake-charmer continued, "The other is made of light; he exudes joy, peace, love, hope, serenity, humility, kindness, benevolence, empathy, generosity, truth, compassion and faith. The same fight rages inside you – as it does for everyone." The grandson thought about it for a minute and then asked his grandfather: "Which cobra will win?" The snake-charmer simply replied, "The one you feed."

The story continues with the snake-charmer replying, "If you feed them both, they both win." He looks at the young boy's puzzled face and continues, "You see, if I only choose to feed the cobra made of light, the one made of darkness will be hiding around every tree waiting for me to lower my guard. It does this to get the attention it desires. His lot in life compels him to live in anger and remain in constant combat with the cobra made of light. By acknowledging him, both cobras remain content and we all win."

As the young boy absorbed the information, the grandfather continued, "For the cobra made of darkness has many attributes that are necessary for us to live full and courageous lives. He provides tenacity, courage, fearlessness, strength of will and great strategic thinking – that we require at times and that the cobra made of light lacks. He makes up for that deficit with empathy, caring, strength and the ability to act for the good of all."

Finally, the grandfather said, "You see, grandson, the light cobra needs the dark cobra and vice versa. To feed only one would starve the other and they will become uncontrollable. To feed and care for both means they will serve you well and do nothing that is not a part of something greater, something good, something of life. Feed them both and there will be no more internal struggle for your attention. And when there is no battle inside, you can listen to the voices of deeper knowing that will guide you in choosing what is right in every circumstance. Peace, my son, is the Hindu mission in life. One who has peace inside has everything. One who is torn apart by the battle within has nothing. How you choose to interact with the opposing forces within you will determine your life. Choose wisely between: starve one or the other and guide them both."

How should we feed our "cobras"?

Feeding the dark cobra requires very little thought. We live in a world surrounded by temptation and unfortunately negativity. Succumb to these and the dark cobra becomes stronger, however, he never becomes satiated. In fact it is quite the opposite. Once his appetite has been stirred he becomes a voracious glutton seeking more. Undoubtedly we all find it easier to feed the dark cobra. His palate is much less discerning than the cobra born of light. He is only too happy to gobble up the perpetual scraps from the table of our baser emotions. Too often anger, jealousy and insecurity appear as our default reactions.

It takes discipline and work to cultivate the behaviors that feed the light cobra. Through acts of kindness, selflessness and justice, the light cobra thrives, guiding us to ever greater vistas of self actualization. The caveat arises when we must confront the stark reality that frequently it appears easier to do the opposite. This however is an illusion. It only appears easier to opt for the path of lesser resistance. Invariably this will manifest in karmic debt and unforeseen problems which ultimately make this path steeper and more difficult to traverse.

How do you feed your friend the dark cobra? Carefully and sparingly. Recognize that since perfection is a myth we cannot expect to behave perfectly all of the time. Whether it is something as relatively benign as eating a piece of cheesecake when dieting, over consuming alcohol or actions that are far more pernicious, we must see them for what they are. These may be symptoms of some anxiety, discontent or a coping mechanism attempting to mitigate feelings of discomfort. Taking a moment to recognize these actions for what they are is the first step to controlling the dark cobra's energy source. At times it may be unavoidable or a conscious choice that leads us to behavior that the light cobra eschews, and the dark cobra chews.

Humans are imperfect and behave in self-serving and petty ways from time to time. The secret is identifying these moments and the catalysts which initiate them. Strive to live your best, respect yourself and others. Although you keep the light cobra nourished, acknowledge your dark cobra and allow yourself a little well-earned fun to maintain and balance your sanity.

SEIZE THE MORNING

Early to bed and early to rise makes a COBRA wealthy, healthy and wise. All right, maybe the quote went a little differently but American founding-father and OG COBRA, Benjamin Franklin, definitely knew what he was talking about. I'm sure you're familiar with the Latin phrase *"Carpe Diem"* which means seize the day. I prefer *"Carpe Mane"* which translates to seize the morning. It's one of the biggest factors I attribute to my success; the ability to dominate the morning. A few hours of solitude allow you to avoid the feeling of being rushed and will reduce your stress dramatically. This in turn can positively change the trajectory of your day. Waking up early, you have yet to be bombarded by the external chaos of the day and was an added benefit, it increases productivity.

Simply waking up early isn't enough. If it were, every little kid who races to the kitchen Saturday morning, grabs a bowl of sugary cereal, and plants themselves in front of the TV to watch four hours of cartoons would be a captain of industry. You need to have a structured, morning routine in place and should be tailored to your life. What works for me may not work for you. For instance, many people like to exercise in the morning and I think that's awesome. I prefer to exercise during the day. This allows me to take an hour for myself, and reinvigorates me. That's what works for me. If your morning exercise is a necessity for you then that needs to be a cornerstone of your morning routine. However, there are certain things that I do that I know will greatly benefit you even if our lives differ. Take what works for you and leave the rest.

HYDRATE

The first thing I do every morning is drink a large glass of water, this accomplishes several important things. Assuming you've slept, (which in some cases can be a big assumption, you know who I'm talking to), your body has gone without hydration all that time and was probably sweaty at some point too, which can leave you a little "dry". Even mild dehydration can affect your

168

brain function and impede mental performance. Coffee is not the answer, despite it being a liquid, the caffeine makes dehydration worse. So, first water, then coffee. Try it, what have you got to lose? Besides isn't your brain important? Give your kidneys a break, they're critical in the process to eliminate toxins, (aka your bad behavior clean-up crew). Take care of the little guys and they'll take care of you with weight loss and healthy, clear skin.

Speaking of weight loss, a glass of water 30 minutes before breakfast tricks your body into feeling fed. If you're anything like me when you wake up, you're ready to feed the machine. Drinking water first is a great strategy to keep the beast in check by avoiding ravenous overeating or eating junk because it's faster. If you're in a hurry, which you shouldn't be if you took my advice to wake up early, any water is better than none. So do what you can... progress not perfection.

Drinking water in the morning is a great way to get a jump-start on ridding yourself of "dragon breath." Dry mouth is the number one cause of bad breath, poor dental hygiene and can lead to tooth decay. Trust me, everyone will appreciate the effort, especially your significant other. If you don't have one, I'm not saying your stink-mouth is the problem, but it isn't doing you any favors. So take a few sips while you swipe right.

GRATITUDE

I like to begin each day in a state of gratitude and humility. Take the time to visualize all the blessings in your life, savor the feeling, this may be the only time you feel kindness all day. This is one of those times you can follow the advice of my wise COBRA wife, Michele :

SPEND A FEW MINUTES FEELING GOOD ABOUT
   YOURSELF SO THAT YOU DON'T SPEND THE
   REST OF YOUR TIME SEEKING OUT THINGS
          TO MAKE YOU "FEEL GOOD"...

like candy, booze, and other vices. The most effective way for me to accomplish this is to get on my knees and communicate with my creator. For you, it could be making a mental list of thank yous to your parents for raising you or a mentor for inspiring you. This is not a theological discussion, take what works for you and leave the rest.

MEDITATE

Next, a brief period of meditation. This silences the distractions from the outside world and the monkey chatter inside your head. Meditation centers you and puts you in a winning head-space. My meditation lasts approximately five minutes and I silently repeat my mantra again and again. Mantra is a Hindu word which refers to a sound, word or series of words that enhance the ability to concentrate and focus. The words which you meditate upon repeatedly will infiltrate your mind and soul and eventually your behavior will express them. Choose them carefully. As a little side note I like to use the A.I. in my phone as both a timer and a source of calming music.

"YOU HAVE POWER OVER YOUR MIND - NOT
OUTSIDE EVENTS. REALIZE THIS AND YOU
WILL FIND STRENGTH."
- MARCUS AURELIUS

VISUALIZE

I visualize the day in front of me. Generally, my schedule for the day is set the previous night. In the morning I make notes concerning any meetings, appointments, chores or obligations that I have during the day. This may involve gathering information about people I will be meeting for the first time. I'm a big fan of intel, do some research. What are the person's interests? Where did they go to school? Can you find any common denominators that will allow you to create a bond with them?

If I'm traveling to a place that I've never been before for a meeting, I will make sure that I know exactly where I'm going. Check if there's road construction or anything else that increases your travel time. There's nothing worse than getting lost on the way to a meeting and arriving frustrated and in a negative head-space.

REMEMBER THE FIVE P'S: PRIOR
PREPARATION PREVENTS POOR PERFORMANCE.

I also visualize the positive outcome that I expect from each of those events. Take a moment and create a video in your mind taking you from the beginning to the end of any important meeting or task. Doing this reinforces a positive attachment in your brain and increases your chances of success. Top-tier athletes do this all the time. Professional sports teams spend big dollars to hire psychologists and motivational specialists to achieve this very thing.

Pitchers visualize the mechanics of throwing the ball with the result of striking out the batter. Batters visualize knocking the leather off the baseball being thrown at them driving it deep into the bleachers. This applies to basketball players, football players, soccer players, etc. I'm not really sure about curling

MAKE LISTS

I'm a big fan of making lists and believe that hand writing them is highly effective. There is something about writing things down by hand that creates a firmer psychological bond than simply entering them into an E calendar on your smartphone. I do both. My smartphone keeps me organized with alerts. The lists I make on legal pads keeps me connected to the task. My legal pad is never out of reach. It serves as a constant reminder of the things that I intend to accomplish during the day. I know that I'm going to have to look at that legal pad later that evening and I don't want to see anything that hasn't been accomplished. This means that I have to carry it over into the next day and I'm already starting the next day with an obligation that will take time away from my objectives tomorrow. Besides, there is something gratifying about ripping off the sheet, crumpling it up and tossing it into the trash... COBRAs toss it from the free-throw line.

Again do what works for you. My wife happens to be a lot more technically inclined than I am. She is a big proponent of using those electronic pens to write on her iPad. She's also one of the most productive people I've ever met, sometimes I swear that she is part machine. We both do basically the same thing but in ways tailored to what works best for us. And trust me, my wife is a queen COBRA.

JOURNALING

Journaling is an extremely effective tool. Stream of conscious writing allows you to get your thoughts, feelings and emotions out of your head and onto the paper without the barrier of self censorship. It's also a great way to quickly improve your mood by expressing difficult and painful subjects you may not be able to share with anyone else. Although you will still have to solve the problems, the act of writing down emotionally charged thoughts can be very freeing. Thus opening you up to other possible solutions that would have been overlooked by your stressed mind. Think of it as Spring cleaning for your soul.

Once you have finished de-cluttering your mind onto the paper, you can burn, trash or keep them. Journals serve as a historian for your life and allow you to periodically return, read the words that you wrote and see where you were and how you felt at a particular time. You can also track your progress and refer back to see how you've dealt with certain issues.

"THERE'S NOTHING TO WRITING. ALL YOU DO IS SIT DOWN AT A TYPEWRITER AND BLEED."
-ERNEST HEMINGWAY

As with anything, the first step is the hardest. If you've never written before it may seem a little touchy-feely for you. I assure you that journaling will not instantly turn you into a sixth grade, school girl writing entries into her diary. You don't need to jump in headfirst, put your foot in the pool. Journaling isn't something that you have to do daily. Try doing it twice a week for five or 10 minutes. It may be for you and it may not. I know that it has been invaluable for me at certain points in my life although I don't do it regularly. It does remain an effective tool in my arsenal to combat anxiety and emotional overload. Plus, it's a lot cheaper than therapy.

Don't get hung up if your writing doesn't look like beautiful Calligraphy. My penmanship resembles that of a doctor suffering from post-hangover shakes. Remember, this is for you. If and when you decide to write your memoirs you can convert it to something more legible.

READING

Reading is one of the greatest equalizers in the world. It doesn't matter where you come from or what your socio-economic background is or even if you were incarcerated. Everyone has the opportunity to travel to exciting and distant locations, learn the thoughts of great artists, generals, actors, scientists and philosophers. All of this can be achieved in the comfort of your home or your prison cell through the pages of a book.

"READING IS TO THE MIND
WHAT EXERCISE IS TO THE BODY."
-SIR RICHARD STEELE

Make a list of subjects that interest you and research books corresponding to the subjects. Take thirty minutes in your morning routine and read. Take that time to learn something that is out of your wheelhouse, out of your comfort zone and that will challenge you. A COBRA may not have a formal education but that doesn't stop you from being well read and conversive in a wide variety of subjects. Reading in silence with a cup of coffee, tea or scotch may grow to be one of your favorite pastimes. By the way, if you're having scotch in the morning you may want to look at some of your life choices. No judgment. Just saying.

After you have completed your morning routine, go out and kick some ass. Forget what happened yesterday, don't stress about what might happen next week and live in the present. The greatest thing about owning the morning is that it is full of possibility. Every new day represents a new opportunity to succeed. Nothing is impossible. The secret is to be better today than yesterday.

FIND A MENTOR

"WE MAKE A LIVING BY WHAT WE
GET.
WE MAKE A LIFE BY WHAT WE
GIVE."
-WINSTON CHURCHILL

As a young boy growing up in a small town in Western Pennsylvania I often sought escape and refuge at the local movie theater coupled with the perfect popcorn/Milk Dud ratio. Nestled in the comforting darkness, I admired the larger than life characters portrayed on the big screen. Whether it was Clint Eastwood as the gritty outlaw Josie Wales, Bruce Lee in *Enter the Dragon* or Alec Guinness as the wise Obi-Won Kenobi. These were my earliest mentors. In retrospect they lead me to pursue a career in acting, study martial arts and eventually become a mentor myself. Eventually I replaced them with people who personally challenged me. Achieving success does not come easily, finding a competent mentor can make all the difference between mediocrity and excellence.

With very few exceptions and throughout history most successful individuals have benefited greatly by having a mentor. Whether it was Plato and his student Aristotle or Warren Buffet and Bill Gates, the list is endless. Although subjected to a contentious apprenticeship, even a renaissance COBRA like Michelangelo labored under the artistic tutelage of Florentine painter Domenico Ghirlandaio who laid the foundation for some of his future work.

The benefits are enormous. Mentors offer real life experience and battle-tested wisdom as opposed to book knowledge. Don't get me wrong, there is much to be learned from books. I hope you agree as you read this one. However, there exists little substitute for the guidance imparted by someone who has already traveled the path you seek. They have probably made many of the mistakes and encountered some of the pitfalls that would otherwise await you. A great mentor holds his mentee accountable, setting goals and reaching them in a timely fashion. More likely than not your trajectory toward success will not always occur vertically. Setbacks and even painful defeats are often part of the journey.

A mentor offers encouragement and occasionally functions as a coach who will pick you up, dust you off and throw you back in the game.

Networking serves as another invaluable asset that a mentor should provide. We have all heard the saying, "It's who you know." These words bear a great deal of validity. The doors that a mentor can open for you may prove an invaluable shortcut to success saving precious time. Learn to stand on the shoulders of giants. The view affords you an enhanced perspective allowing you to see the "lay of the land" rather than merely the immediate road before you.

Mentors may be found in many different places. Look for them where you work, where you play and where you study. Find an individual who has achieved that which you strive to achieve. If you still find it difficult to locate a mentor you may consider looking online. There are numerous organizations which assist in placing mentors and mentees together. Look on social media platforms like LinkedIn, Instagram and Twitter.

"IF YOU CANNOT SEE WHERE YOU ARE GOING, ASK SOMEONE WHO HAS BEEN THERE BEFORE."
- J. LOREN NORRIS

Once you find someone that you believe would be a good fit, do some light background research on them. Investigate their education, professional history, interests, hobbies and any other information that will allow you forge a meaningful and constructive relationship. Just be careful not to overstep by invading their privacy, you're not the CIA. No one wants to mentor a creeper... cyber-stalking is a fine line to walk. The best strategy is to take it slow and see if your personalities mesh well.

Next ask them if they have the willingness and availability to mentor you. Also, be certain that you are willing and able to dedicate the necessary time that would be required of you. A mentor has the responsibility of acting as a steward to the success of his mentee. However, a good mentor should make it very clear that he or she will not work harder than their mentee.

Communication is paramount. Start by conveying what it is you want to accomplish. Come to a prospective mentor with very clear ideas of what you hope to gain from the relationship. Then ask what your perspective mentor can offer and help the best like to work and communicate. Some people like to meet in person, others prefer email while still others prefer using the phone.

Consistency is critical. Try to set up a weekly time when you and your potential mentor can communicate. Most likely your potential mentor has a very busy life. It's imperative you respect their boundaries and determine a set of guidelines that will govern how you interact with each other.

RESPECT is one of the five pillars of the *Way of the Cobra*. Remember the saying,

YOUR LACK OF PLANNING DOES NOT
CONSTITUTE ANOTHER PERSON'S EMERGENCY.

Late night or repetitive calls to a mentor is a sure fire way to torpedo the relationship. Always be respectful of your mentor's time. A COBRA values the time of others and as such is never late. In fact, in this dojo, if you're not early, you're late.

A mentor functions as a guide and a sounding board but not a crutch. Be certain that your newfound mentor is willing and able to effectively convey their experience and wisdom. Lastly remember that as you achieve your success you have a responsibility to pay it forward. Be ready. At some point someone may ask you to act as their mentor.

"SERVICE IS THE RENT YOU PAY FOR YOUR
ROOM HERE ON EARTH."
-MUHAMMAD ALI

APOLOGIZING

"SOME PEOPLE ACCIDENTALLY WALK
ON YOUR FEET AND APOLOGIZE,
WHILE OTHERS WALK ALL OVER YOUR
HEART AND DON'T EVEN REALIZE."
- UNKNOWN

When a COBRA is in the wrong they apologize sincerely and as soon as possible. We do this not simply to convey remorse to the other person but also to free ourselves. Failing to apologize when you are at fault and know it produces negative energy in the form of destructive guilt and remorse, blocking happiness and productivity. This will keep you from manifesting your highest self, enjoying your best life and releasing your inner masterpiece, plain and simple. This doesn't mean that you can't function or achieve sporadic moments of success but know this: You will not achieve your full potential. If you can live with that then skip this part. In fact, skip the rest of the book. You still with me? Good. I'm proud of you. I knew you had the makings of a true COBRA.

Guilt and remorse are not completely useless emotions. They are useful tools serving a specific function. Remorse occurs when we genuinely feel sorry for actions and behavior for which we feel responsible. Remorse acts as a barometer letting us know through emotional discomfort when we have behaved in a way that violates our personal values and/or those of society. Getting bombed at the office holiday party and insulting your bosses' taste in neckties tends to leave a pretty nasty psychic hangover to accompany the physical one. Not to mention it doesn't put you at the top of the promotion list. It doesn't take a rocket scientist to know that probably wasn't your finest moment. Not apologizing however makes the situation exponentially worse.

You may already feel remorse but now guess who's coming to dinner like a pair of obnoxious party crashers unwilling to leave? Say hello to guilt and his BFF shame. These guys will keep harassing you until you take action to rectify or repair the situation with an apology. By the way, you may want to pump the brakes on the Johnny Walker.

177

You know that nagging heaviness that keeps dragging you back to the past like a bad credit score at the new car lot? Guilt. We become stuck We find ourselves spending more time replaying events from the past than living in the present. That negative mental loop erodes your confidence and keeps you from ascending toward your higher self. The only thing guilt is good for is feeding your inner critic, so fix it and starve the little bastard. Apologizing allows you to let go of the debilitating bondage of guilt. I'm not going to lie to you. You may still feel remorse but apologizing will reduce your feelings of guilt because you have taken action. You have enough distractions vying to live rent free in your head without cluttering it with psychic and emotional trash caused by guilt and living in the past. Keep your mind clear so that your thoughts and abilities can flourish.

The willingness to apologize when necessary represents one of the most effective tools to "let go"of anxiety, doubt and guilt. It also conveys RESPECT which is an integral pillar in the *Way of the COBRA*. This brief story that illuminates the wisdom of letting go. The power to do so is invaluable.

A soft mist hovered above the ground. The two Chinese monks, one the older master and the other the young student, had walked for some time in contemplative silence as they made their way back to the distant monastery. It had rained the day before and the country road was covered with puddles. At a certain point they reached a ditch filled with water from the rain. While neither deep nor wide it was impossible to continue on without wading through the water. The monks soon realized that they were not alone. A beautiful girl stood at the edge of the gully afraid to make her way through the water. After a moment the elder monk approached her. He gently lifted her in his arms, walked stalwartly ahead and gently placed her on the other side of the road. He then continued on his way to the monastery.

The next day the younger monk came to the cloister of the elder monk and said, "Master, you know better than I that we monks have sworn an oath of chastity and it is forbidden for us to touch a woman." The elder monk responded "Yes, brother." Then the younger monk inquired yet again, " But master, how is that you lifted that woman on the roadside?" The wise monk smiled, "I left her on the other side of the road, why are you still carrying her?"

Stop carrying around your guilt. The key to accomplishing

that is, you guessed it, _APOLOGIZING_! Bold, underlined and in italics. Clear enough for you? I know. Easier said than done. Why is it so difficult to apologize? Somewhere in your life you associated saying "I am sorry" with weakness. That somehow, admitting you are wrong, behaved poorly or hurt somebody diminishes you as a person. Let's be clear. You probably already took care of that with whatever you did that requires an apology. Apologizing ain't gonna make it worse. You need to comb the sands of your memories and uncover when, where and why this happened. Once you locate the accurate and honest circumstances and events of the moment that affected how you view apologizing, you need to deconstruct it. Ask yourself the following questions:

☐ Was I too young to properly interpret the situation?

☐ Did someone with negative intentions influence me?

☐ After apologizing, was I derided, criticized or ridiculed?

☐ Was I raised that emotionality equaled weakness?

Any of these could lead to negative, unproductive and false stories about apologizing that hold you back. We humans, and at the risk of sounding misogynistic, especially men, have a great deal of difficulty with words that come in threes: "I love you," "I need help," and "I don't know." Most of us learned that nonsense about the same time we were told boys don't cry and finish all the food on your plate. This genius advice spawned a generation of emotionally repressed over eaters but I digress.

On the contrary, offering a sincere apology demonstrates strength and security. Obtaining forgiveness shouldn't be your goal. If you are fortunate enough to receive it you will lighten your emotional and psychic burden. You want to bust out of the emotional block of marble that's holding you back? Do you want to chisel away all of the extraneous and debilitating crap that only holds you back? Then kick your ego to the curb, put on your big boy or girl gi and make with the apology.

I could say something fancy like "the chasm between the desire to say 'I am sorry' and taking action to do so causes tremendous anxiety and distances you from your authentic self and the emergence of your inner badass." That would certainly be an accurate and keen observation. But it's actually much simpler. Knowing you should apologize and not doing it happens for two reasons:

1. Your big fat ego gets in the way.
2. YOU ARE ACTING LIKE A CHICKEN AND NOT A COBRA!

Stop getting tangled up in the results that an apology may or may not produce. Stay in the present of the apology itself and the rest will unfold as it will. Apologizing presents the opportunity for a win-win scenario. Apologize honestly and with the sincere intention of reconnecting with the other person. It may have the desired effect and maybe it won't but at least you are taking proactive and positive action. You must in turn be willing to accept this, learn from your mistakes and move forward. Likewise, the act of forgiveness goes a long way to free the injured party who often shoulders the burden of anger, resentment and frustration. Apologizing offers them the chance to let go of their baggage, releasing the emotional attachment that binds them to your damaging transgression. This smooths the path to healing. It's a win-win.

Circumstances may preclude you from apologizing because the intended recipient has passed away. The next logical course of action, if and only if, appropriate is to offer the apology to the family. Sometimes the best way to make reparations is through living amends. This means that you live your life in a way that demonstrates integrity and awareness so as to never repeat the previous mistake and serve as an example to others.

The way you apologize is every bit as important as what you say. Our society feeds on nano-second sound bites like the commercials created by Madison Avenue advertising agencies. Thanks to technology we have achieved modes of communication which provide us with greater levels of productivity and convenience. Often however the trade off for convenience and speed comes in the form of detachment. Communications philosopher Marshall McLuhan wrote in his book, *Understanding Media: The Extensions of Man*, that

"THE MEDIUM IS THE MESSAGE."

McLuhan believed that the way in which a message is disseminated carries more importance than the very message itself. Unless you have a communications degree or are a Woody Allen fan, you may not be familiar with him but the guy was on to something. McLuhan appears in Annie Hall and lambastes a pompous television media professor who loudly and incorrectly espouses McLuhan's thesis while in line at a movie theater. McLuhan fixes his little wagon but good.

If you seriously want to apologize then pay special attention to the way you deliver it. Electronic mail, text messaging and to a lesser degree telephone calls imply a conscious or subconscious desire to detach and create distance from the person who you are trying to connect. If possible apologies should be conducted face to face. Don't be that person that communicates critical emotional information with a Post-It note on the fridge. On a selfish and somewhat paranoid level remember that the internet lives on forever. Before you email anything, you would be wise to remember that with a keystroke, it could be available for the world to see.

An apology is not primarily for or about us. It is not about defending or explaining our intentions, feelings or character. Do not frame the apology in a passive voice. Saying "I am sorry you were offended" does not constitute a sincere apology but only seeks to shift the blame and onus. As an added bonus it makes you sound like a self-righteous jerk. The sole goal and intention of an honest apology centers around the other person's feelings. The ultimate objective should attempt to heal the hurt and loss of connection that our actions and words caused.

A simple and concise way to apologize:

1. Express remorse, say "I'M SORRY."
2. Take responsibility, say "I WAS WRONG."
3. Be specific, say "I DID X and Y."
4. Make amends, ask "WHAT CAN I DO TO FIX IT?"
5. Put the amends into action.

Start scrolling through your mental and emotional files. Pull up the people with whom you need to apologize. Do it. Take action right now.

• List situations which require an apology.

Write down to the best of your ability all of the circumstances that you remember including who, what, when and where. Specificity and clarity will help the authenticity of your apology.

• List negative consequences from not apologizing.

• Make an action plan to communicate the apology.

Remember, meeting in person is always best. If distance truly presents an insurmountable obstacle then ask if the recipient would be willing to do a video call. It's very likely that they may still be angry, hurt, or disappointed by your actions. Be very specific when reaching out that it is your only intention to offer an apology. If they are unwilling to communicate with you then ask if they would allow you to send a handwritten apology letter.

- Now, right now, take action.

In creating this list do not forget to include yourself. I wager that you have done or said hurtful things to yourself that require an apology and clear the road for you to forgive yourself and your inner child. For many years I detested my younger self. I viewed him as weak and a victim. Apologizing to that fat awkward kid and in effect myself has helped me tremendously. I told him that I was sorry that I couldn't protect him, that I couldn't shield him from pain and humiliation. In turn he forgave my adult self which has allowed me to heal that part of me.

This is the power of apology. This is how you start chipping away the emotional negativity that imprisons your masterpiece. The only question resides in whether you want to use a hammer and chisel or a pen knife.

OWN YOUR FEELINGS

By this time in the book, you've got some pretty good tools to work with but... you are still feeling emotional pain. Sometimes it comes out as sadness other times it explodes into anger. It's because your Dark Cobra hasn't been fed yet. Now's your chance. Make a list of everyone who has hurt you... go as far back as you can remember. Make sure you write down exactly what they did and why. How it made you feel and what you did, if anything, in response. Now for the good part, feed your Dark Cobra, imagine what you would do to each one of them if you could. Get it all out...channel Darth Vadar as you write:

"HARNESS YOUR ANGER LUKE. COME OVER TO
THE DARK SIDE."

Now seal that paper in an envelope and put it somewhere safe. (If you did it right, it would not be interpreted well by anyone that found it.) Set a reminder on your calendar to open it in two weeks. While we wait, let's acknowledge that there are two kinds of people in the world: people who have experienced some form of abandonment, neglect, rejection, or abuse in the past; and liars. I don't have to read your list to know that you are no exception and COBRAs aren't liars. Everyone has trauma but who you blame for it depends on how well you feed your Dark Cobra. Yeah, I said blame. You believe your current emotional state is someone's fault. Could be people from your past, like your parents, caregivers, exes or even you.

As long as you look for blame, you are keeping yourself in victim mode. VICTIMS DO NOT EXIST IN OUR DOJO! Assigning blame is a waste of time. No one can make you feel anything, you are the only one who controls your emotional responses. If you are experiencing pain it originates from the stories that you are clinging to. If you're not clear about the power of stories, reread the section Power of Story.

Do you get angry when someone at work talks to you in a short way? Or is there someone at work you just can't stand? Come on COBRA, you're not really angry, or at least not at them. Cue Freud: it's your subconscious mind rehashing old patterns that were never corrected. Most likely it was a parent or teacher who frightened you or upset you when you were a tiny white belt unable to defend yourself. Time to settle the score COBRA, you don't have to confront the original offender (unless you want to), but you do need to confront the story you are clinging to. It's the real culprit in this scenario. So take to pen and paper to feed your Dark Cobra by having the entire confrontation, do you your worst. DO IT! Now it's time to let go now by creating new patterns and associations. As long as your focus is on blaming your past, others, or God for your pain, you have no power to do anything about it. You will always be at the mercy of what other people do or don't do for your happiness and peace of mind if you focus on blame and you will not heal from your past.

Let's start at the beginning, I promise I'm not going to interpret your dreams, but I am borrowing a page out of Freud's book because, despite his prodigious appetite for cocaine, he was onto something with his examination of parental relationships. Let's be honest, no one escapes childhood unscathed. If you have kids of your own, you are on the road to recovery. Children serve as a cypher to unlock the reasons our parents did what they did or didn't do. (If they are your biological children, they are a magnifying glass to your childhood horrors because they inherit your personality traits and you got yours from your parents...) Feed your dark COBRA by writing out the whole argument, point by point, once and for all with your parents. Air every grievance, name their favorite child, pull the string that will unravel the whole sweater that is your parental relationship. Now, breathe. Take a break. Get some water... NOT FIRE WATER, alcohol has no place in this exercise. Now re-read what you wrote and decide whether you are going to confront your parents or just burn it. COBRAs realize that our parents are flawed, but so are we. Your mom doesn't go to this dojo so it's time to clip the umbilical cord of negative stories and start fresh with yourself in the driver's seat of curating your self-esteem.

Later in life, you fell in love with someone, only to be hurt when that person betrayed your trust in some way ending the relationship. The ghost of your first love is scarier than The Conjuring. It leaves you terrified to get hurt again so you hide the real you, especially if they show the slightest sign of being cold or distant. Your current relationships, form a pattern... dare I say a script... cue the un-dead guy with a chainsaw. Something happens that "triggers" a subconscious memory of your past horror. Say your partner laughs with an acquaintance at a party. You see this, and instantly you just about want to crawl out of your skin as you hum the theme song from Psycho to pace yourself while you devise an excruciating way to dispose of the acquaintance.

It's like deja vu all over again. Doesn't your partner understand how hurtful they're being, especially given your past? It's like they're trying to cut your abused heart out of your chest. You've invented new angry curse words to spit at your partner and, ya know what? Your ex should get an earful too... if you can locate that home wrecker.

Tap the brakes COBRA. I'm about to drop some knowledge: you are the problem, but not in the way you think. Don't get me wrong, your cheating ex is a terrible person for hurting you, but their complete lack of ethics and selfish actions led you to believe that you aren't worthy of a partner's fidelity therefore you must force it by implementing Mossad level hyper-vigilance. When you see your partner enjoying someone's company, you choose to interpret that as history repeating itself because you have lost your ability to be impartial. You can't possibly be objective given your underlying belief that the only way to be sure your partner is faithful is to kill everyone around them. COBRAs do not require orange prison jumpsuits to gain perspective. Feed your dark COBRA by enjoying the rest of the party. On the drive home, tell your partner that you were delighted to see them laughing because they deserve to relax and have fun after how hard they worked all week. If that doesn't do the trick then guess what? It's time to write another letter, the dark COBRA takes a while to feed into submission.

Don't forget to open your letter from two weeks ago. Read it in a calm happy place with fresh eyes. Once you realize how silly some of your gripes are, dismiss them. For the others, decide your next course of action carefully. Either burn the letter and the emotion attached to it or confront and overcome, but it's time to move on COBRA, your inner badass is released.

COBRA RELEASED

"Now this is not the end. It is not even the beginning of the end, but it is, perhaps, the end of the beginning."
                              -Winston Churchill

A central facet of my personal life philosophy mandates that I make myself available to help others in my everyday life. It's largely why this book is extremely important to me. I believe in the transformative nature of these words. I believe that through my experiences I am in a position to help many of you while simultaneously helping myself. Although we have come to the end of this book, our journey together is far from over. We are now bonded together. While you are my student, you are also my teacher. Make no mistake, I have learned a great deal from you, thank you.

You have worked diligently and have hopefully discovered exciting new things about yourself. You have learned to view not only the world differently but also your place in it. As a COBRA you now have the responsibility to make our world a better place. Earning your place as a COBRA in our dojo is not easy. Maintaining it is even more difficult. In order to do so you must take what you have learned and create the life you deserve. In doing so you will shine like a beacon to those around you, hopefully illuminating the path for them to do the same. I have faith in you.

Congratulations! You are well on your way to earning your black belt in the Way of the COBRA. Remember that this is simply another step in a journey that lasts a lifetime. Now you are ready to learn.

Our deepest fear is not that we are inadequate, our deepest fear is that we are powerful beyond measure. It is our light, not our darkness, that most frightens us.

We ask ourselves, who am I to be brilliant, gorgeous, talented and fabulous? Actually, who are you not to be? You are a child of God. Your playing small doesn't serve the world. There's nothing enlightened about shrinking so that other people won't feel insecure around you.

We were born to make manifest the glory of God that is within us. It's not just in some of us, it's in everyone. And as we let our own light shine, we consciously give other people permission to do the same. As we are liberated from our own fear, our presence automatically liberates others.

1994 Inaugural Speech of Nelson Mandela

Invictus

By William Earnest Henley

Out of the night that covers me,
Black as the pit from pole to pole,
I thank whatever gods may be
For my unconquerable soul.
In the fell clutch of circumstance
I have not winced nor cried aloud.
Under the bludgeoning of chance
My head is bloody, but unbowed.
Beyond this place of wrath and tears
Looms but the Horror of the shade,
And yet the menace of the years
Finds and shall find me unafraid.
It matters not how strait the gate,
How charged with punishments the scroll,
I am the master of my fate,
I am the captain of my soul.

The Road Not Taken

By Robert Frost

Two roads diverged in a yellow wood,
And sorry I could not travel both
And be one traveler, long I stood
And looked down one as far as I could
To where it bent in the undergrowth;

Then took the other, as just as fair,
And having perhaps the better claim,
Because it was grassy and wanted wear;
Though as for that the passing there
Had worn them really about the same,

And both that morning equally lay
In leaves no step had trodden black.
Oh, I kept the first for another day!
Yet knowing how way leads on to way,
I doubted if I should ever come back.

I shall be telling this with a sigh
Somewhere ages and ages hence:
Two roads diverged in a wood, and I—
I took the one less traveled by,
And that has made all the difference.

DO NOT GO GENTLY INTO THAT GOOD NIGHT

By Dylan Thomas

Do not go gentle into that good night,
Old age should burn and rave at close of day;
Rage, rage against the dying of the light.

Though wise men at their end know dark is right,
Because their words had forked no lightning they
Do not go gentle into that good night.

Good men, the last wave by, crying how bright
Their frail deeds might have danced in a green bay,
Rage, rage against the dying of the light.

Wild men who caught and sang the sun in flight,
And learn, too late, they grieved it on its way,
Do not go gentle into that good night.

Grave men, near death, who see with blinding sight
Blind eyes could blaze like meteors and be gay,
Rage, rage against the dying of the light.

And you, my father, there on the sad height,
Curse, bless, me now with your fierce tears, I pray.
Do not go gentle into that good night.
Rage, rage against the dying of the light.

IF *by Rudyard Kipling*

If you can keep your head when all about you
*   Are losing theirs and blaming it on you,*
If you can trust yourself when all men doubt you,
*   But make allowance for their doubting too;*
If you can wait and not be tired by waiting,
*   Or being lied about, don't deal in lies,*
Or being hated, don't give way to hating,
*   And yet don't look too good, nor talk too wise:*

If you can dream—and not make
dreams your master;
*   If you can think—and not*
make thoughts your aim;
If you can meet with Triumph and Disaster
*   And treat those two impostors just the same;*
If you can bear to hear the truth you've spoken
*   Twisted by knaves to make a trap for fools,*
Or watch the things you gave your life to, broken,
*   And stoop and build 'em up with worn-out tools:*

If you can make one heap of all your winnings
*   And risk it on one turn of pitch-and-toss,*
And lose, and start again at your beginnings
*   And never breathe a word about your loss;*
If you can force your heart and nerve and sinew
*   To serve your turn long after they are gone,*
And so hold on when there is nothing in you
*   Except the Will which says to them: 'Hold on!'*

If you can talk with crowds and keep your virtue,
*   Or walk with Kings—nor lose the common touch,*
If neither foes nor loving friends can hurt you,
*   If all men count with you, but none too much;*
If you can fill the unforgiving minute
*   With sixty seconds' worth of distance run,*
Yours is the Earth and everything that's in it,
*   And—which is more—you'll be a Man, my son!*

THANK YOU

Understanding who we are and how we can best serve the world is not a solitary journey. We meet many fellow travelers along the way. The influence they imprint upon us is sometimes fleeting, but in the most fortunate instances endures. Each of you have touched, changed and improved my life. With love, humility and boundless appreciation I thank you for all you have bestowed upon me especially my fans who, without you, I wouldn't be where I am; my family what, without you, I wouldn't be who I am; my friends who, without you, I wouldn't be who I am, and my wife who, without you I wouldn't have a how or why. If I have accidentally neglected to list anyone below, you are not forgotten nor is your contribution any less appreciated. You have my word as a **COBRA**, I will make it up to you on the website.

Sensei Chad Addis, John G. Avildsen, Eva Basler, Charlene Bazarian, Susan Bernhart, Bradley Bell, Robyn and Mike Bernstein, Eleo Bettencourt, Matthew Blondell, James Cullen Bressack, Sarah Joy Brown, Karl Bruen, Grant Butlin, Marlo Capps, Tanya and James Blake Coscia, Simone Danker, Gabriela Delgado, Master Fumio Demura, Pablo Diez, Lauren DeNormandie, Peter DiNovi, Michael Fairman, Sensei William Christopher Ford, Laura and James Franklin, Jason Gonzalez, Rob Grace, David Greer, Josh Heald, Carolyn Hennesy, Jeff Hill, Jon Hurwitz, Dimitri James, Pat Johnson, Charli Kanan, Michele Kanan, Peter Kanan, Karen Krasney, Pierpaolo Lazzarini, Dr. Robi Ludwig, Ashley and Daniel Jacobs, Dr. Mary and Geoffrey Keyes, Annie and Bradley Keyes, Alma and Dr. Sidney Keyes, Ilona Koti, Martin Kove, Michael James Lazar, Jill Liberman, Shelley and Frank Litvack, Roy London, James Lott, Jr., Adam McKinley, Ralph Macchio, Domenico Mazzella, Michael Maloney, Giulio Montanaro, Pat Morita, Deirdre and Greg Morris, Melissa Neiderman, Diane and Andrew Neiderman Roger Newcomb, Markos Papadatos, Michele and Dale Perelman, Janice and Lawrence Perelman, David Perelman, Jennifer Perelman, Joe Peri, Pew$, Connie Pfieff, Will Roberts, Anthony Robbins, Teresa and Tristan Rogers, Marco Antonio Rota, Ron Russell, Connie and Adam Saunders, Hayden Schlossberg, Adrian Sifuentes, Carlos Siquero, Pjetur Sigurdson, Tom Stacy, Jimmy Starr, Sensei William Stoner, Tracy Swope, Rabbi Pinchas Taylor, Angie Theo, Maria Theo, Ron Thomas, Anthony Turk, Anne-Sophie Vega, Giovanna Vega, Juliet Vega, Doug Vermeeren, Darryl Vidal, Cathea Walters, Timothy Woodward, Jr., Ariel Yariv, William Zabka.

ABOUT THE AUTHOR

Transform yourself and you can transform the world.

SEAN KANAN

A true renaissance man, Sean Kanan epitomizes the expression "triple threat" having achieved success as an actor, producer and author. Sean's first book, The Modern Gentleman: Cooking and Entertaining with Sean Kanan received rave reviews. His second book, Success Factor X, became an Amazon new release best seller one week after its release and was recently named one of the twenty most inspirational books in the last two decades by Book Authority. Sean has been interviewed numerous times by everyone from FOX Business anchor Maria Bartiromo to Katie Couric.

Sean's acting career exploded with his breakout performance as a villain, Mike Barnes, in the The Karate Kid III beating out over two thousand hopefuls in an open call to his iconic award winning roles in daytime television playing black sheep AJ Quartermaine on General Hospital to his critically acclaimed portrayal of Deacon Sharpe on The Young and the Restless and The Bold and the Beautiful, television's most syndicated show in history seen in over one hundred countries. Having appeared in more than one thousand episodes of network television and fifteen feature films, Sean is recognized around the world. Most recently Sean has created and stars in the critically acclaimed and Emmy award winning, digital series, Studio City exclusively on Amazon Prime. Sean is very active in numerous charitable organizations including The American Cancer Society, various animal advocacy groups and serves as the youth ambassador for Boo2Bullying. Sean earned a bachelors degree in political science from UCLA. Whether through his acting, writing, speaking or coaching Sean loves inspiring people and is passionate about making a difference in the lives of others. Sean and wife, Michele, split their time between Los Angeles and Palm Springs where he has a star on the walk of fame. He spends his free time practicing martial arts, cooking, traveling and studying multiple foreign languages including Italian and Mandarin.